The Highest In Us

The Highest In Us

TRUMAN G. MADSEN

Bookcraft
Salt Lake City, Utah

Library of Congress Catalog Card Number: 77-93271
ISBN 0-88494-334-8

3rd Printing, 1980

Lithographed in the United States of America
PUBLISHERS PRESS
Salt Lake City, Utah

Contents

Preface

"There are no ordinary people," C. S. Lewis writes. Instead we "live in a society of possible gods and goddesses. The dullest and most uninteresting person you talk to may one day be a creature which, if you saw it now, you would be strongly tempted to worship, or else a horror and a corruption such as you now meet, if at all, only in a nightmare."[1]

The nightmare is all about us. And as we peer out at the world, whether by the aid of television or not, there is much of horror and of corruption. Yet, on occasion, quiet voices remind us, against all evidence to the contrary, that there are "overwhelming possibilities" locked within mankind.

What we see of potential in others we see only dimly in ourselves, in spite of much that is in the air about attitudes and positive thinking. One of our own classic LDS sources says we must view ourselves, in our carnal state, as less than the dust of the earth. Whatever else that abysmal self-appraisal means, it is at

---

[1]C. S. Lewis, *The Weight of Glory*. (Grand Rapids, Michigan, William B. Eerdmans Publishing Co., 1949), p. 15.

least clear that, unlike those of us who go on postponing response to our better selves, the dust is subject to the will and power of the Master. But what would dust, filled with life and consciousness and glory, be? The very nature of the Master. And here we must see upward in order to see inward. "No being can thoroughly learn himself, without understanding more or less of the things of God; neither can any being learn and understand the things of God without learning himself; he must learn himself, or he never can learn God."[2] Modern prophets, who had not only the image but the vision of the things of God, say, like the Prophet Joseph Smith struggling to describe the majesty of the resurrection, "No man can describe it to you, no man can tell it." Yet, expressible or not, a glimpse is overwhelming. Brigham Young, addressing disillusioned wives, testified, "The transcendent beauty of person, the God-like qualities of the resurrected husband that she now despises, even if she could but see a vision of him," would lead her to "feel like worshipping him, he is so holy, so pure, so perfect, so filled with God."

This collection of essays revolves around the quest to unleash the "highest in us." Its undergirding theme is that the power of God is in places we consistently neglect—in the spiritual sense of our divine origins, in flashes of spirit memories, in the Master's call to expanded and intensified living, in the sacramental approach to daily life, in soul-probing responses to tests like unto Abraham's, in the lucid and time-tested pronouncements of our own conscience, in the privileges of intimate prayer, and in the environs of the link between heaven and earth, the temple.

None of these sources and resources are exhausted in our lives—some remain almost untouched. But the possibilities are there.

On hostile college campuses, as I have learned in recent years, there is much resistance to the Latter-day Saint understanding of

---

[2] Brigham Young, *Journal of Discourses*, Vol. 8, p. 33.

man: that he embodies more than a spark of the divine—that he is, in his potential, the complete flame of God. All the counter-arguments reduce to one: It is a self-serving "stretch" beyond reality; it is too good to be true. Nevertheless, it is true. And this awareness of self in doubt-consuming light, brings what one writer has called the sense of winning the sweepstakes. It releases powers of love and healing and energy and creativity that can be found in no other way.

Needless to say, the readings and interpretations herein, in matters both of history and of doctrine, are my own. I do not speak officially.

My thanks go to Paul Green of Bookcraft, who encouraged me to bring under one cover these presentations, and to a continual flow of students who demonstrate to me that, beyond all the justified pessimism, cynicism and skepticism of our times, there is a way up and out.

—TRUMAN G. MADSEN

The Highest in Us

We begin with an incident from our LDS history which, when I first read it, inflamed me and changed my life. In the 1830s there was a student at Oberlin College, Ohio, whose name was Lorenzo Snow. He was disillusioned with what he saw of religion in general and Christianity in particular. He wrote a letter to his sister who had become a Latter-day Saint, Eliza R. Snow, and confessed his difficulties. She wrote back and invited him to Kirtland. He came. Within a few moments, as I read the story, he was inside the temple, the building which at that time served, as many of you know, more than one purpose. It served *all* of the fundamental functions of the Church. As he entered, there was a small meeting in progress. Patriarchal blessings were being given by the Prophet's father, Joseph Smith, Sr. He listened, first incredulous, then open, and toward the end inspired. He kept saying to himself, "Can this be simply a man or is there something divine involved?" More and more he felt that the Spirit was in it.

Based on an address given at a ten-stake fireside at BYU, March 3, 1974.

At the end of the meeting, the Prophet's father took Lorenzo's hand (there had been no introduction as I read it) and, still filled with the light of his calling, said two things to him. "You will become one of us." Lorenzo Snow understood that but didn't believe it. But now the staggering statement. "And you will become great—even as great as God is. And you could not wish to become greater." Young Lorenzo Snow did not understand that. Shortly the first prediction was fulfilled. His conversion, his baptism and confirmation left him somewhat stillborn. But then came his immersion in the influences of God so that for several nights he could hardly sleep, burning, he says, with a "tangible awareness" of God in a way that changed him.[1]

Move now to a later period in his life. He had served; he had become one of our great and dedicated missionaries. He was sitting discussing the scriptures with a brother in Nauvoo. At that moment something happened to him which in later life he called an impression; sometimes he spoke of it as a vision, and always as an overwhelming revelation. He came to glimpse the meaning of what had been said to him. And he formed it in a couplet which all of us hesitate, and I think wisely, to cite in discussion or conversation but which is a sacred, glorious insight. It's a couplet; he put it in faultless rhythm: "As man now is God once was. As God now is man may become." He says he saw a conduit, as it were, down through which, in fact, by our very nature, by our being begotten of our eternal Parents, we descend and up through which we may ascend. It struck him with power that if a

---

[1]"When the Book of Mormon was first read at my father's, I was struck with favorable impressions; and afterwards on hearing Joseph Smith bear his testimony by the power of the Holy Ghost to its truth, a light arose in my understanding which has never been extinguished." (Lorenzo Snow Journal, handwritten manuscript, p. 1, "Lorenzo Snow papers, 1840-1901," Church Historical Department.)

"I was baptized by John Boynton in June, 1836, and confirmed by Hyrum Smith. I received a knowledge of the divine authenticity of the gospel in the most happy and glorious manner. The heavens were opened and the Holy Spirit descended upon me and I tasted the joys of eternity in the midst of the power of God. Those manifestations have never been effaced from my memory." (Lorenzo Snow Journal, p. 3.)

prince born to a king will one day inherit his throne, so a son of an Eternal Father will one day inherit the fulness of his Father's kingdom.

Suddenly he recovered the New Testament verses, repeated but without depth, in which we are commanded to become perfect. (Then, lest we should relativize that, the Master had added, "even as your Father.") The verses in 1 John vibrate with John's comprehension of love: "Behold, what manner of love the Father hath bestowed upon us, that *we* should be called the sons of God. . . . Beloved, now *are we* the sons of God, and it doth not yet appear what we shall be: but we know that, when he shall appear, *we shall be like him*; for we shall see him as he is." (1 John 3:1-2. Italics added.)

The concept became a guiding star to young Lorenzo Snow. It went with him through other callings and sacrifices. He hardly dared breathe it—even to his intimates—except to his sister, Eliza, and later during a close missionary discussion with Brother Brigham Young. Not a word had been spoken by the Prophet Joseph specifically giving that principle, but Lorenzo knew it. And you can imagine how he felt when, in the Nauvoo Grove in April 1844, the Prophet Joseph Smith arose and said with power, "God was once a man as we are now."

Now may I take you elsewhere to sympathize for a moment with the outlook others have on this and to understand why our concept is sacred and must be kept so. In a discussion at a widely known theological seminary in the East, I was asked, "What is the Mormon understanding of God?" I struggled to testify. Then three of the most learned of their teachers, not with acrimony but with candor, said: "Let us explain why we cannot accept this. First of all, you people talk of God in terms that are human—all too human." (That's a phrase, incidentally, from Nietzsche.) "But the second problem is worse. You dare to say that man can become like God." And then they held up a hand and said, "Blasphemy."

Well, that hurts a little. I was led to ask two series of questions. (Mind you, I'm telling you the story. I'm not sure they would tell it the same way. I've had a chance to improve it in the interim.) The first was a series of questions about the nature of Christ. "Was he a person?"

"Yes."

"Did he live in a certain place and time?"

"Yes."

"Was he embodied?"

"Yes."

"Was he somewhere between five and seven feet in height?"

"Well, we hadn't thought of it, but, yes, we suppose he was."

"Was he resurrected with his physical body?"

"He was."

"Does he now have that body?"

"Yes."

"Will he always?"

"Yes."

"Is there any reason we should not adore and honor and worship him for what he has now become?"

"No," they said, "he is very God."

"Yes," I said, "what then of the Father?"

"Oh no, oh no!" And then they issued a kind of Platonic manifesto—the statement out of the traditional creeds which are, all due honor to them, more Greek than they are Hebrew. "No, no, the Father is 'immaterial, incorporeal, beyond space, beyond time, unchanging, unembodied, etc.' "

Now, earlier they had berated me because Mormons, as you know, are credited—or blamed—for teaching, not trinitarianism, but tritheism—the idea of separate, distinct personages in the Godhead—and denying the metaphysical oneness of God. I couldn't resist at this point saying: "*Who* has two Gods? You are the ones who are saying that there are two utterly unlike persons.

The religious dilemma is, How can I honor the Father and seek to become like him (for even the pronoun *him* is not appropriate) without becoming *un*like the Christ whom you say we can properly adore and worship and honor?" Well, the response at that point was that I didn't understand the Trinity. And I acknowledged that was true.

But now the second set of questions: "Why," I dared to ask—and it's a question any child can ask—"did God make us at all?" There's an answer to that in the catechisms. Basically, it is that God created man for his own pleasure and by his inscrutable will. Sometimes it is suggested that he did so that he might have creatures to honor and worship him—which, if we are stark in response, is not the most unselfish motive one could conceive. Sometimes it is said that he did so for *our* happiness. But because of the creeds it is impossible to say that God *needed* to do so, for God, in their view, is beyond need. And then the bold question I put was "You hold, don't you, that God has and had all power, all knowledge, all anticipatory wisdom, and that he knew, therefore, exactly what he was about and could have done otherwise?"

"Yes," they allowed, "he could."

"Why, then, since God could have created co-creators, did he choose to make us creatures? Why did God choose to make us his everlasting inferiors?"

At that point one of them said, "God's very nature *forbids* that he should have peers."

I replied: "That's interesting. For us, God's very nature *requires* that he should have peers. Which God is more worthy of our love?"

Now, as Latter-day Saints we know that prophets have lived and died to reestablish in the world in our generation that glorious truth—that what the Eternal Father wants for you and with you is the fulness of your possibilities. And those possibilities are infinite. He did not simply make you from nothing into a worm; he adopted and begat you into his likeness in order to share his nature. And he sent his Firstborn Son to exemplify just how glorious that nature can be—even in mortality. That is our witness.

In all things, Lorenzo came to wonder why others did not wonder at this. "Nothing," he said about three months before his death, "was ever revealed more distinctly than that was to me. Of course, now that it is so well known, it may not appear such a wonderful manifestation, but when I received it the knowledge was marvelous to me." (*Church News*, April 2, 1938.) Modern revelation, in ways even Latter-day Saints take for granted, had taught clearly that Jesus the Christ exceeded mankind in every way and was unique in that he was the Firstborn, and the Only Begotten in the flesh, and the only sinless man and therefore "wrought out the perfect atonement through the shedding of his own blood." (D&C 76:69.) The atonement was and is perfect because it empowers mankind for a perfect work: perfection. Christ's mission was to overcome the vast difference between his nature and blessedness and our own. Thus he came to accomplish, in the language of a modern scholar, "the universal divinization of man." That we might understand how to worship and know what we worship, the following great kinships of destiny are taught in the Doctrine and Covenants. (I have made some minor modifications of wording in the quotations given.)

I was in the beginning with the Father. (93:21.)	Ye were also in the beginning with the Father. (93:23.)
I am the Firstborn. (93:21.)	All those who are begotten through me are partakers of the glory of the same [the Firstborn], and are the church of the Firstborn. (93:22.)

[I] received not of the fulness at first, but continued from grace to grace, until [I] received a fulness. (93:13.)

I . . . received grace for grace. (93:12.)

I . . . received a fulness of the glory of the Father. (93:16.)

[I] received a fulness of truth, yea, even of all truth. (93:26.)

The glory of the Father was with [me] for he dwelt in [me]. (93:17.)

[I] received all power, both in heaven and on earth. (93:17.)

[I] . . . ascended up on high, as also [I] descended below all things, in that [I] comprehended all things, that [I] might be in all and through all things, the light of truth. (88:6.)

[My] light shineth in darkness, and the darkness comprehendeth [me] not. (88:49.)

Ye must grow in grace and in the knowledge of the truth . . . you shall receive grace for grace. (93:20.)

You may come unto the Father in my name, and in due time receive of his fulness. (93:19.)

He that keepeth [my] commandments receiveth truth and light, until he is glorified in truth and knoweth all things. (93:28.)

If you keep my commandments you . . . shall be glorified in me as I am in the Father. (93:20.)

[You are] possessor[s] of all things; for all things are subject unto [you], both in heaven and on the earth, the life and the light, the Spirit and the power, sent forth by the will of the Father through Jesus Christ his Son. (50:27.)

The day shall come when you shall comprehend even God, being quickened in him and by him. (88:49.)

If your eye be single to my glory, your whole bodies shall be filled with light, and there shall be no darkness in you; and that body which is filled with light comprehendeth all things. (88:67.)

Glory be to the Father, and I partook and finished my preparations unto the children of men. (19:19.)

[I] shall reign for ever and ever. (Revelation 11:15.)

King of kings and Lord of lords. (Revelation 19:16.)

[Ye] shall be priests of God and Christ, and shall reign with him. (Revelation 20:6.)

[He] hath made us kings and priests unto God and his Father. (Revelation 1:6.)

He that receiveth me receiveth my Father; And he that receiveth my Father receiveth my Father's kingdom; therefore all that my Father hath shall be given unto him. (84:37-38.)

[Ye] are priests of the Most High, after the order of Melchizedek, which was after the order of Enoch, which was after the order of the Only Begotten Son.

Wherefore, as it is written, they are gods, even the sons of God—

Wherefore, all things are theirs, whether life or death, or things present, or things to come, all are theirs and they are Christ's, and Christ is God's.

And they shall overcome all things.

Wherefore, let no man glory in man, but rather let him glory in God, who shall subdue all enemies under his feet. (76:57-61.)

Christ, Paul testified, "thought it not robbery to be equal with God." Modern prophets thought it not blasphemy to be "joint heirs" with Christ.

But how can all this relate to the pronouncements of scripture that man is, in his raw and rudimental state, "carnal, sensual, and devilish"; that man must come to see himself as "even less than the dust of the earth"? (The dust, at least, abides the measure of its creation. Not the earth but the inhabitants thereof pollute and abuse and "hate their own blood.") Is not the tenor of the scriptures ancient and modern that we must become as little children and, in the depths of humility, "consider ourselves fools before God," and that otherwise we are "despised" and the Lord will not open unto us?

More than once in heady circumstances such statements have been thrown up to us, especially from those of the "neo-orthodox" tradition in theology which holds, in the spirit of Augustine, Calvin, Barth, Brunner, and Reinhold Niebuhr, that Mormons are afflicted with a triple and fatal pride—a pride of Church status, a pride of self-righteousness, but worst of all a pride of aspiration.

Lorenzo Snow found his answer in Christ the Exemplar:

Jesus was a god before he came into the world and yet his knowledge was taken from him. He did not know his former greatness, neither do we know what greatness we had attained to before we came here, but he had to pass through an ordeal, as we have to, without knowing or realizing at the time the greatness and importance of his mission and works." (Office Journal of Lorenzo Snow, 8 October 1900, pp. 181-182, Church Historical Department.)

Lorenzo Snow had no doubt that we are dependent upon the Lord for life itself and utterly dependent upon the Lord Jesus Christ for eternal life. Yet he could say, "Godliness cannot be conferred, but must be acquired." (Eliza R. Snow Smith, *Biography and Family Record of Lorenzo Snow* [Salt Lake City: Deseret News Company, 1884], p. 193: hereafter cited as *BFRLS*.)

And cannot such aspiration be selfish? Not for him. No man understood better than he that in order to be and become like the Master one must submit and surrender. Thus he wrote, "The Priesthood was bestowed upon you, as upon the Son of God, for no other purpose than that through sacrifice you might be proven, that, peradventure, at the last day, you might stand approved before God, and before perfect and holy beings, and that in order to merit this divine approval, *it may be necessary to forget self and individual aggrandizement and seek the interest of your brethren.*" (*BFRLS*, pp. 376-377. Italics added.)

When the Prophet first presented to him the law of eternal marriage, Lorenzo shrank and said he felt to fear that he could not live this principle in righteousness. The Prophet Joseph replied (confirming what Lorenzo Snow had wondered about in his own spirit): "The principles of honesty and integrity are founded within you and you will never be guilty of any serious error or wrong, to lead you from the path of duty. The Lord will open your way to receive and obey the law of Celestial Marriage." (*BFRLS*, p. 70.) And so he did. There is something autobiographical in his comment, "I have known individuals who have trembled at the idea of passing through certain ordeals who after they were through the temptation said they could approach the Lord in more confidence and ask for such blessings as they desired." And then he added:

Every man has got to learn to stand upon his own knowledge; he cannot depend upon his neighbor; every man must be independent; he must depend upon his God for himself entirely. It depends upon himself to see if he will stand the tide of trouble and overcome the impediments that are strewed in the pathway of life to prevent his progress. A man can get information by the operations of the Holy Spirit and he approaches to God and increases in his faith in proportion as he is diligent. (Gems of Truth, *Millennial Star*, December 10, 1888, p. 806.)

The light of the Holy Spirit, as Brigham Young once said, lighted up his weaknesses as well as his strengths. (It is no contradiction to say that the greater our vision of possibilities, the greater our consciousness of present weaknesses.) During the "reformation" era in the Church, when all the Brethren were asked to reexamine and probe and purify their lives, Lorenzo Snow with his friend Franklin D. Richards finally came to feel that they were unworthy of their high callings. The two went together to President Brigham Young and offered to give up their priesthood and their standing in the Twelve. "I guess there were tears in his eyes when he said, 'You have magnified your priesthood satisfactorily to the Lord.' " (See *Southern Star*, Vol. 2, p. 39.)

As the demands of discipleship descended upon Lorenzo he recapitulated the struggle of righteous men of every generation. The "why me?" that many ask in the hour of tragedy was coupled with "why me?" in the presence of great blessings. He heard the Prophet witness that the nearer one comes ·to living celestial law the greater the opposition to be expected.

But instead of seeking to become a man of Bunker Hill (as in the children's game, "I'm the boss of Bunker Hill, I can fight and I can kill") in an unlicensed will to power (in some dominant, Hitlerian sense) it was for Lorenzo Snow just the other way:

There is just one thing that a Latter-day Saint, an Elder in Israel should never forget: it should be a bright illuminating star before him all the time—in his heart, in his soul, and all through him—that is, he need not worry in the least whether he should be a deacon or President of the Church. It is sufficient for him to know that his destiny is to be like his Father, a God in eternity. He will not only be President but he may see himself president of a Kingdom, president of worlds with never-ending opportunities to enlarge his sphere of dominion.

I saw this principle after being in the Church but a short time; it was made as clear to me as the noon day sun. . . .

This thought in the breasts of men filled with the light of the Holy Spirit, tends to purify them and *cleanse them from every ambitious or improper feeling.*

This glorious opportunity of becoming truly great belongs to every faithful Elder in Israel; it is his by right divine and he will not have to come before this or any other quorum to have his status defined. He may be a God in eternity; he may become like his Father, doing the works which his Father did before him and he cannot be deprived of the opportunity of reaching this exalted state.

I never sought to be a Seventy or High Priest, because this eternal principle was revealed to me long before I was ordained to the Priesthood. The position which I now occupy [he was then President of the Church] is nothing as compared with what I expect to occupy in the future. (At a meeting of the First Presidency in the Council of the Twelve, recorded in BYU Special Collections, Microfilm Reel number 1, page 209. Italics added.)

My testimony to you is that you have come literally "trailing clouds of glory." No amount of mortal abuse can quench the divine spark. If you only knew who you are and what you did and how you earned the privileges of mortality, and not just mortality but of this time, this place, this dispensation, and the associates that have been meant to cross and intertwine with your lives; if you knew now the vision you had then of what this trial, this probation (what in my bitter moments I call this spook alley) of mortality could produce, would produce; if you knew the latent infinite power that is locked up and hidden for your own good now—if you knew these things you would never again yield to any of the putdowns that are a dime a dozen in our culture today. Everywhere pessimism, everywhere suspicion, everywhere the denial of the worth and dignity of man.

I have faith that if we caught hold of God's living candle on that truth and went out into the world—I don't care if the vocations concerned are sensational, spectacular, or brilliant—just out in the world being true to the vision, we would not need to defend the cause of Jesus Christ. People would come and ask: "Where have you found such peace? Where have you found the radiance that I sense in your eyes and in your face? How come you don't get carried away with the world?" And we could answer that the work of salvation is the glorious work of Jesus Christ. But it is also the glorious work of the uncovering and recovering of your own latent divinity.

I know that idea is offensive to persons whom I would not wish to offend. I know that it goes against the grain of much that is built into our secular culture. I know that there are those who say there is no proof. But I bear witness that Jesus Christ, if there were none else, is the living proof, and that, as you walk in the pattern he has ordained, *you* will be living proof. I bear that witness in the name of Jesus Christ. Amen.

Freedom to Become

My wife, Ann, and I had the privilege not long ago of visiting Hong Kong, that little, jutting segment of China which does not really belong to the new China but which is still under British rule, and where many Chinese have come for political asylum. We met many of some four thousand who had recently become Christians—Latter-day Saints—most of them under the age of thirty. Not a few of them had come from Red China. They first came for only one reason—freedom.

As we stood at the border, which is carefully marked, and saw the small river that separates the two realms, we inquired quite naively: "Well, why don't people just walk over? We don't see anything to prevent it." (We'd heard of the bamboo curtain but we couldn't see any bamboo.) It was explained to us that no one, not even a mouse, could cross there. It was mined; it was watched; it was guarded like a prison yard. And if anybody thought that he

Address given at an investigator fireside at Oakland Interstake Center, July 28, 1973.

could get out of Red China and into Hong Kong there was only one way today—a marathon swim. He had to go out into the ocean a great distance in cold and sometimes shark-infested water, and then he had to make a kind of a moon-shaped swim and come back in—sometimes swimming as much as twenty-five miles. No sane person would begin that swim unless he knew he could stay in the water for at least a day and a half. That's why those who made it were young.

The week we were there we met a man whose relative had made that attempt only a week before. This man started with thirteen others. People know before they begin that their odds for survival are one in ten. When patrol boats spot them, they're simply shot. (The bodies roll up onto Kowloon Peninsula every day.) The men in this particular group went without food for five days before they began to swim. (That was because if they had asked for food it might have been suspected what they were about.)

Of the thirteen, three made it, one of them the man whose relative we met. We learned from him that there had recently been a couple who set out for freedom and the Communists had shot the husband when they were four miles away. Apparently the patrol unit didn't recognize that there were two swimmers. So the wife, in the manner of lifesaving swimming, then pulled her husband's body the rest of the way so he could be buried on free land!

Now, I believe in freedom and I believe freedom is worth sacrifices. And I believe America is great, if it *is* great at all, because blood has been shed not only to buy freedom here but to hold to it elsewhere. But that's freedom *from*. That's freedom *from* intimidation; freedom *from* a police state; freedom *from* external pressures and dominations.

There's another kind of freedom. That is freedom *for* something. Freedom to *become* what you have it in you to become. Sometimes you don't have to be free *from* in order to be free *for*.

Christ became what he is while being denied most of the freedoms you and I have in this country. The Prophet Joseph Smith grew most at times when he had the least freedom *from*. He experienced a tremendous soul growth during a six-month period when he was in jail—much of that time in a jail ironically called Liberty. Freedom to *become* matters even more than freedom *from*.

Now, will you forgive me if I confide in a personal manner a story which has gripped me more than I can say? It is a story by James Hilton, the author of *Goodbye, Mr. Chips* and of *Lost Horizon*, the man who created the beautiful myth of Shangri La. James Hilton wrote another book called *Random Harvest*. Many years ago a film version of that book was made starring Ronald Coleman and Greer Garson.

The story is about a wealthy and titled Englishman who goes to war and in the midst of a battle is, as they used to say, "shell-shocked" by an explosion. His memory is blotted out. He doesn't even know his own name. And further, his speech is impaired to the point that under any pressure he can hardly say a word. They bring him back to England and put him in an asylum. He stays there in the hope that his parents—he doesn't know *who* they are—will come and inquire and tell him who he is. He yearns to belong to someone. Many couples come. All turn away immediately, disappointed.

The war ends and in a pea-soup fog he walks out of the asylum—no one guarding, all are celebrating—finds himself hustled and bustled in the crowd, and comes into a little shop. There he meets Paula, a beautiful woman who immediately recognizes that he is from this hospital. Out of sympathy and with a certain amount of courage she cares for him. In due time his stutter passes a bit and he begins to find himself. He aspires to be a writer on a shoestring and they marry and subsequently have a son.

One day (you feel a little ominous about it as you see the movie) he's saying good-bye to her, their first parting since marriage. He's going into the big city to deliver a manuscript. In

Liverpool he is struck by a cab, and all of his former memory of his identity comes back. But he is blank from the moment of shell shock; which means he cannot remember meeting Paula or any of the subsequent events.

Now what? Well, that's the rest of the story. The point here isn't just that this is a great love story (for it is that); it's that it is the symbol—the allegory—of our lives. And I'll explain in a moment how deeply the allegory applies.

He goes back to his family home, Random Hall, becomes successful in business, and runs for Parliament. The doctors advise Paula that there is no way she can jog or shake him into remembering her, but she loves him so deeply that eventually she applies successfully to be his secretary. There are moments when he stares at her and asks questions. She *knows* he's on the verge of recall, but always, disappointingly, he turns away and says something like, "Well, you know how people have feelings that they have known someone before."

Then the plot thickens; he proposes marriage—but only a state marriage, only a social-secretary arrangement, what he calls "a merger." "No emotional demands," he says. Again the doctor advises her "No," ("You're going to be hurt") but she can't help herself, and she becomes a kind of wife. The climax of their difficulty is the night that he presents her with an incredibly beautiful emerald, but as she goes into her room and opens the drawer, there is the little bit of cheap jewelry that he had given her as "Smithy" (that's what she called him). Somehow the value of those beads over the value of the jewel pierces her heart and she cries out, "Smithy!" He discovers her in this condition and wonders aloud if he should have "interfered in her life." Paula laments: "The best of you, your capacity for loving, your joy in living are buried in a space of time you've forgotten." She is resolved to leave him, perhaps for good.

Just before her departure he travels on business to Melbridge, the same community where the asylum is. He assumes he's never been there before. He takes care of his business, but, walking with a friend, he says, "Let's go into this little shop." And the friend asks, "How did you know there was a little shop of this description?" "I don't know, I . . . I *did* know! But I don't know how!" Memories begin to flow. Shortly he finds his way back to the asylum. "I remember I was here. I came out of these gates." His friend says, "Let's retrace your steps, then."

Now comes the climactic scene. (And I have read somewhere that Greer Garson says that of all the parts she ever played in life as well as in Hollywood, no scene overwhelmed her as did this one.) He goes back to the cottage where he lived with Paula as Smithy. All the time in the interim he has carried the key in his vest pocket. Now he is back to the door where he had waved good-bye that morning. He walks to the gate; it still squeaks in the same way. He walks under the buds of a tree; they have a familiar look. The key fits, and the door swings open. Now Paula, who has heard that he is in the area and is hoping against hope that he will remember her, rushes up to the gate. He turns around. The question is, will she say, "Smithy," or will she say, "Charles"? She risks it. She says, "Smithy." He looks confused. She says it again and breaks into tears. He still looks confused. And then the camera comes in close and you see in one radiant wave the whole past come to his face. In an instant he recovers himself, his past, and his beloved. "Paula!" And they rush into each other's arms. That's the end. It's also the beginning.

What does that story have to do with freedom and fulfillment? What does it have to do with *you?* So much! So much.

We, too, are wealthy and titled "Englishmen." We once dwelt in the scintillating presence of the Eternal Father. So rich, so exquisite was our condition there (though it was not without conflict), that we can hardly endure remembering. Wilford Woodruff heard the Prophet Joseph Smith remark that were it not for the strong biological urge in us to survive, to hold on to the slipping rope even when we are in pain and suffering, and, in addition, were it not for the veil of forgetfulness, we could not stand this world. Our mortal amnesia is the Lord's anesthesia. We must stay in this condition to work out our possibilities, undergo the stress and distress that lead to perfection.

One role of the Christ, as of his prophets, is to remind us—to "bring all things to our remembrance." (See John 14 and Diary of George Laub, BYU Special Collections, pp. 9-16.) Brigham Young taught that we are totally familiar with God the Father, but that knowledge is "locked up" within us. Nothing, he said, will so much astound us "when our eyes are open in eternity, as to think that we were so stupid in the body." (See Harold B. Lee, *Youth in the Church* [Salt Lake City: Deseret Book Co., 1970], p. 50.) Lorenzo Snow taught that "according to our preparation there"—and he taught that our preparation was exactly suited to our anticipated missions—"our flesh was to become acquainted with our experiences in the spirit."

Like Sir Charles Rainier in the story, we were sent into the mortal world clear in the vision of how high were the stakes. (There is a real evidence that some shrank from that momentous decision.) And we, too, have been shell-shocked. We do not now know our own name, rank, and serial number. Even the memory of a perfect language, with its grace and ease and instant communicative power, is gone. Here, we do indeed stammer and stutter in speech as in conduct, groping our way to self-understanding and feeling at times, even in the midst of helpful people, "strangers and foreigners." We yearn to belong. Only when we are touched by the Spirit do we overcome, for a fleeting time, our memory imprisonment. Then, as Joseph F. Smith puts it, "we are lighted up with the glory of our former home."

And there are other wonderings. Why are we drawn toward certain persons and they to us, as if we have always known each other? Is it a fact that we always have? No matter if the "parties are strangers," Parley P. Pratt observes, "no matter if they have never spoken to each other. Each will be apt to remark, 'Oh, what an atmosphere encircles that stranger. How my heart thrilled with pure and holy feelings in his presence. What confidence and sympathy he inspired.' " (*Key to Theology*, 7th Edition, [Salt Lake City: Deseret News Co., 1915], p. 96.) "If the ties of this world will extend to the next, why not believe," Orson F. Whitney asks, "we had similar ties before we came into this world . . . some of them at least?" "I have this belief concerning us," says George Q. Cannon, "that it was arranged before we came here how we should come and through what lineage we should come. . . . I am as convinced that it was predestined before I was born that I should come through my father as I am sure that I stand here." (George Q. Cannon, *Utah Genealogical and Historical Magazine*, Vol. 21, 1930, p. 124.) The Prophet Joseph Smith confided to his intimates that we had some choice as to the time and the family of our mortal sojourn, he having chosen his parents.

"I believe that our Savior is the ever-living example to all flesh in these things. He no doubt possessed a foreknowledge of all the vicissitudes through which he would have to pass in the mortal tabernacle. . . . If Christ knew beforehand, so did we." (Joseph F. Smith, *Gospel Doctrine*, 8th Edition [Salt Lake City: Deseret Book Co., 1949], p. 13.) Through the perceptions of prophetic men we are told the day will come when we shall recognize, as Orson Pratt wrote, that every spirit of man saw Christ in the premortal councils. And in the resurrection: "Then shall ye know that ye have seen me, that I am, and that I am the true light that is in you, . . . otherwise ye could not abound." (D&C 88:50.)

The language of the literary world preserves something of the premortal sense. Plato's classic myth in the *Symposium* teaches (some think only playfully) that the soul lived in a perfect world, directly aware of the true, the good and the beautiful; that lovers were there entwined in a metaphysical unity. In this present world, learning is but recollection. We search in vain for self-understanding until we encounter our exact counterpart, our "other half," our mate. Then our capacity for love expands and we relive the intense passional echoes of that relationship. In finding our companion or companions we literally find ourselves.

The myth is contained, with profound Christian overtones, in the newly discovered apocalyptic writings of upper Egypt. We know now that there were many forms of Gnosticism, but some of them contained elements of New Testament truth. It is taught in one form of Gnosticism that the fall of man was estrangement from woman and the glorification of man is sacred marriage, the reunion of the separated in the mergings of the "bridal chamber," which is the highest sacrament. Eve, whatever her role in man's fall, is a partner with Christ in his redemption.

We have flashes—the French phrase is *déjà vu*, which literally translated means "already seen." We cry out, "I have anticipated this." And there are other wonderings—haunting landscapes, the sounds of music that are echoes of eternity, a love for the truth ("my sheep know my voice"), and spiritual acquaintanceship. We only skim the surface in our seekings, yet we do not trust the psychologists who tell us that we use less than 5 percent of our potential. We doubt the studies of aptitude and talent that show that we are, each one of us, in a unique way, geniuses. In the struggle to communicate, to decide, to plan, to express creative talent, to forecast, to cope with learning challenges, we often consider ourselves "behind," "backward," and "just average." But the prophets teach us that "to every man is given a gift," and, as Orson Pratt put it, no one is left destitute. Joseph Smith taught that we cannot receive more until we honor what has already been given. We have great gifts, greater endowments, and the greatest of destinies. The gold is in the mine. But the power of Christ must sink a shaft to bring it out. In the end our becoming depends on pre-tastes or, quite literally, after-tastes.

A morning is ahead when there will be brightness and glory exceeding all prior mornings, and a "perfect bright recollection." Then, we are promised, we will be given back our lost memory and with it our selves. The key will fit the door. As the earth will become an instrument of truth whereby "all things for our glory, past, present and future" will be manifest, so we will become living Urim and Thummim. We will not just begin to see. We will see it all. "The day shall come when you shall comprehend even God, being quickened in him by him." To comprehend God is to comprehend all that God comprehends, to "see as [we] are seen and know as [we] are known." (D&C 76:94.) If in this world our spirits still sing in the afterburn of that exposure, how, "with spirit and element inseparably connected," we shall sing a new, more glorious song in his eternal presence! Surely a climactic scene awaits all of us.

I Am the Life

E ducation Weeks are a baptism of fire. The instructions seem easy enough: Just condense a whole semester's course into three hours, expect an average of three hundred students per class, teach three to four classes in a row, live out of a can, and, oh yes, teach like Karl G. Maeser! I recall overhearing a colleague of mine discussing the resurrection. He made the point that many prophets have said that there are essential elements in our bodies which will never become an essential part of any other and which will be reunited with our spirits in the resurrection. Someone asked him, "What are the fundamental elements?" He thought for a moment and said: "Go and see Truman Madsen. He's down to them already."

In this and other ways I've been accused of being undernourished. In self-defense I have said that there is nothing in the scriptures that provides for the survival of the fattest. Seriously, I have on occasion wanted to say to these many choice people who

---

Address given at BYU Education Week devotional, 1973.

come to Education Week—come hungering and thirsting, some of them giving up vacations, sleeping in cars, going without—a sentence spoken by Christ himself anciently: "I have meat to eat that ye know not of." The most exhausting and most exhilarating teaching challenge of my life has been Education Week.

The spirit may be strong even when the body is weak. A few blocks from here is a home and a bedroom where, even as I speak to you this morning, there is a boy sixteen years old, slowly dying. In his infancy he was normal, healthy, bright-eyed, promising; but then the processes began to reverse in him. (There's a technical name for the affliction—Herler's Syndrome.) Since eight-and-a-half or nine he has been bedfast, and he has long been immobile. It is inadequate to say he is only skin and bone—he is hardly that. He has not enough muscle left even to clear his throat, and only enough consciousness to recognize his mother, she thinks. The fading vital signs diminish the hope that he will live much longer. Asked to administer to this youngster, I faced the strange dilemma as I placed my hands upon him: to whom am I speaking? And there came over me a feeling that locked within this racked body was a giant of a spirit. Almost the feeling of a musical genius struggling to perform on a battered, stringless instrument. And as I sought to make promises, and then, trembling, left the home with the bishop, I became conscious in ways I cannot put into words that there is meaning in the sentences, "I am the life," and "I am the resurrection and the life."

The Lord Jesus Christ in all his teaching presupposes that he has somehow gained power over all the powers of life, that all things, both in heaven and in earth, are subject unto him. Professor Hugh Nibley, who has just read a thousand books in order to write one, tells us that in most ancient world religions—Greek, Roman, Oriental, Phoenician, Hebrew—the temple was symbolic of the very navel of the universe, the life link between heaven and earth. The temple is the house of the Lord

Jesus Christ. That insight becomes exponential when you think that he has also told us in modern revelation "man is himself a temple—a living temple." To cut or to poison that channel is to begin to die. To have health, wholeness in it is to begin to live.

A graduate student and a lover of comparative literature was assigned recently to go through the Doctrine and Covenants and look for what we called "image families." His quest: To what illustrations does the Lord over and over resort in revelation? You who have read the book, could you guess? There are three that dominate all others. They are: light and darkness, planting and harvesting, and lifting and raising up. The biological analogues are photosynthesis, growth, and fruitfulness. And at the very center of those images used so often is the image of birth and rebirth. The Lord says in that glorious prose poem, Doctrine and Covenants 93, "All those who are begotten through me are partakers of the glory of the same." He is the Firstborn. We, through him, though we be lastborn, are yet partakers of the glory of the Firstborn. The word *glory* itself has a constellation of connotations—life, spirit, power, light, fire.

It was the Prophet Joseph Smith who taught us that we must have a kind of new birth even to *see* the kingdom of God and recognize that we are somehow out of it. Then we must be born of water and of the Spirit in order to *enter* it. And just as that is central to all his teaching, it is central to all the ordinances of the gospel which take the life-giving elements—for example, the water, the bread, the oil—and enable us to particpate in the process of divine nourishment.

Students constantly corner me and ask, "Dr. Madsen, do you believe there are any absolutes in this universe of ours?" (They have been taught that all absolutes are obsolete.) I answer, "Yes." They challenge, "Name one." Here is one: Life can only come from life. That is an eternal law. There is no other way. You can only be born by having parents. (Any of you who were born in some other way can be excused from genealogical research.) The

Lord chose the image of begetting to remind us of that central and glorious truth.

Recently I stood in a translating room where words that have been written heretofore in English are now being put into Chinese characters. The mission president confided that he had a real problem with the Doctrine and Covenants. The trouble is the word *quickened*. It is used frequently in modern revelation. But it has no Mandarin or Cantonese synonym. They can come close. There are words that imply motion or function or speeding up. What is missing in any of the attempted words is the idea of animation, of life. It is the word *quickened* that the scripture uses to describe what happened to Adam when he came up out of the water and the power of God centered in him and he was "quickened in the inner man." (Moses 6:65.) "Quickened," the source of life. The Chinese have the life without the word. Perhaps we Americans have the word without the life.

May I apply this insight to some of our ordinary thinking about life in the Church? The Prophet Joseph Smith once compared life to a wheel that each of us move around. There are times when we are up and someone else is down. But in due time it is the other way around. In that setting he added, "Every man [every woman, too] will fail sometime." Hence the need of the Church, that some who are alive and high can lift those of us who are more or less barren, numbed, deadened. If this perspective begins to sink into us, many things take on a different light.

One supreme compliment to a member of the Church is, "He is active." But so are falling rocks and billiard balls. The word the Lord uses, and the question derived from it is, "Are you a *lively* member?" Are you alive?

It's no longer a question of whether you have been through the standard works, but whether the life and light in them has somehow passed through the very skin of your bodies and enlivened you.

It isn't whether you *say* your prayers in a proper fashion and position and time, but whether you open up honestly what is alive and more or less dead within you to the Source of life and stay with it and with him until the return wave of life enters you.

In recent years the Church has set many new attendance records. But how nourished are those who are within the Church buildings?

It's not a question of whether you can show the leaves—go through the motions, if you will—of the religious life. Christ, in what seems to some a most severe act, saw those leaves on the fig tree near Jericho and was convinced thereby that there were figs, whereas actually there were none. And the tree was cursed and henceforth was good for nothing but to be burned. Are you fruitful? Do you bear fruit? That is the question.

"Is he a good speaker or teacher in the Church?" we often ask. How little do our students, our classroom members, understand that most of what happens depends on them. If they come hungering, thirsting, centering their concentrated faith in the person who seeks to speak or teach, they pull out of him the seeds of life and spirit which are then planted in them and grow. This I've come to know as people come forward and thank me for teaching them things that I myself did not know. It is the Spirit that nourishes growth. The teacher only plants.

We stand and testify and speak well about the Lord's menu. But do we deliver the Lord's food—and feed his sheep with heavenly manna?

Are we programming each other (programming can be to death as well as to life)? Or are there dynamic currents flowing through these programs into us?

We "sustain" the Brethren by "voting" for them periodically. But the question is, Do we give them our sustenance? Do we seek assurance that the Spirit of the Lord called this man to his position? Are we willing to exercise our faith and prayers that he may be magnified? If so, both he and we are vitalized.

We have a teacher training program that has been preoccupied, in recent years, with the idea that the classroom experience should change behavior. But the Lord Jesus Christ is far more ambitious for us than that. He wants to change us, to produce celestial personalities. And if we will let him, he has the power. How can any mortal teacher do that? He cannot—unless he has an unimpeded channel to the generator of life, who is Christ. A teacher's greatest success is when his students are tied to Christ. Too many of us are tempted to win *our own* disciples.

Some of us do a "100 percent home teaching." But do we leave in the home a living atmosphere?

What good is a woman, I am sometimes asked, who has done almost nothing for years "except hold a family together"? That is all. The Lord's answer is that if she has created and transmitted the nutriments of spiritual life in her home (and in the early days the Saints always dedicated their home to the Lord), then she has been the purveyor of life. And nothing is more crucial!

Suppose we go to the temple and (how impotent the phrase!) "do names." Actually we are bringing new birth and life to spirit personalities whose exquisite gratitude, according to the Prophet Joseph Smith, will be such that they will fall to our knees and embrace them and bathe our feet with their tears. That is what we are about. And in the well-chosen phrase of Arthur Henry King, we ourselves return again and again to the temple to be born and reborn again and "to resacramentalize our marriage" and our home.

The time may come when we don't just "say a blessing" on the food but when we, in effect, seek to make every act of our lives life-giving and done in the Lord's name and with his Spirit. Then the whole earth and the whole day and the whole of our lives will be the temple within which we labor with and for him.

In short, worship of the Lord Jesus Christ is more than being attracted by his personality, fascinated by his teaching, even desirous of imitating his conduct. That's only part. It is a matter of our coming unto him with all of our life faculties open and receiving his glory—receiving his power and his life.

President Marion G. Romney has borne witness that when section 88 says that there are three different degrees of glory, those degrees are more than orbs or worlds. They are you—your own body. And your glory is to be that glory by which you are quickened *in the present life.* There is therefore a sense in which, as we sit here today, there are three kinds of personality—three different circuits, right here and now—some who are attuned to the celestial life and nourished by it breathe a better atmosphere, sing a richer song, express more powerful forces, and drink and eat a stronger and more heavenly meal. Others of us are still on a lesser circuit, eating husks. Our ultimate glory will depend upon our circuit here.

Now may I take you to a sacred place. There is a garden near some fruitful olive trees in Jerusalem. To it Jesus was wont to go. (The Prophet's verb is "accustomed to go.") On a given night anciently the power of his compassion, the power of his identifying imagination, the power of his sacrificial love began its awful work in his system. As he knelt under the ravages of all the forms of spiritual dying, he cried out for help. Even he? Yes. But was he not one who had moved "from grace to grace," one who had honored always the will of the Father? Did he not have sufficient strength to go through it? Thank the Lord for the message still in the record and left unchanged in the Inspired Version, that even he reached the limit.

Luke records, "And there appeared an angel unto him from heaven, strengthening him." This was the same Christ who had only within days been on the Mount of Transfiguration, having undergone divine manifestations so great that we have not yet been trusted to know all that took place. Yet now the burden became unbearable. And who was the angel? We know there are none who minister to this earth (minister or administer) but those who do belong or have belonged to it. Who was he? And can we believe, though we know not, that the strengthening, the life-giving touch (for it must have been that) was infinitely more than the placing of a moist, cool cloth on a fevered and bleeding brow?

How many of us have been stillborn, are stunted, staggered, barely holding on? But Christ went through what he had to in order to generate in his own center self compassion for us. And to earn everlastingly, and make real to every bit of consciousness throughout all space and time, the power of life!

Now, I pray that we will not be, as were the Jewish leaders and the Romans who stood looking up at the cross, unable really to see, taunting him with words like these: "Come down, you who are so high and mighty; you who have claimed so much; you who have said you could save men and now cannot save yourself. Come down! Prove you are God." Here is the ultimate absurdity of sign-seeking, saying in effect, "We will only believe if you will come off the cross and do external magic." The whole message was that he was willingly *on* the cross to prove forever, and lift us forever toward, the inward power of love and life.

To those of us, then, who thirst, I plead, Come to him. He turns no penitent one away. Would you, if you had paid so much in suffering? Would you ever give up? All doors that are locked against the Lord are locked by us. He is always waiting, promising life where there has been death, healing where there has been sickness, forgiveness where there has been sin. And sin is poison. He sets us all an inversion of our own example. We say to people who have hurt us: "If you will change, I will forgive you—but not until. If you deserve forgiveness, you shall have it." But Christ said to the woman taken in adultery, as he wrote in the sand in the outer court of the temple (the only writing of his that is mentioned in the four Gospels), "Where are thine accusers?" You remember her reply. He said: "Neither do I condemn thee; go, and sin no more." (John 8:10-11, Inspired Version.) The Inspired Version adds a sentence: "And the woman glorified God from that hour, and believed on his name." The offer of forgiveness *before* we have changed in order that we may change—that is the power of Christ. And it brings flowing, living water to the famished soul.

It was John the Beloved (who according to a recently discovered manuscript likely was the youngest of the ancient apostles), a mere boy not yet weathered into cynicism, who stood, you recall, with the mother of Christ before the cross. The only one of the Twelve. Later, having filled a great mission—weathered, but not withered—and having received the revelation that closes the New Testament, he cites the voice of the Lord Jesus Christ in power in the spirit of eternal truth and in glorious poetry. He says: "And the Spirit and the bride say, Come. And let him that heareth say, Come. And let him that is athirst come. And whosoever will, let him take the water of life freely." (Revelation 22:17.)

How more could the Lord have taught us this than when he identified himself over and over with the elements of life?

"I am the living bread."

"I am the true fountain."

"He that believeth on me, as the scripture hath said, out of his belly shall flow rivers of living water. But this [says John] spake he of the Spirit."

"I am the vine."

"Ye are the branches."

"I am the life."

"Without me ye can do nothing."

May God bless us to come hungering and thirsting and receive the birth and rebirth that is in Jesus Christ until we, like him, are "quickened in the inner man."

The Sacramental Life

*L*et me begin with a kind of cross-disciplinary statement about religion. There is a remarkable convergence of ideas about the aspect of religion I want to discuss. Borrowing a phrase from an anthropologist, Clifford Geertz, I speak tonight of "consecrated behavior." What he means by this is so obvious it may elude us:

It is in some sort of ceremonial form, even if that form be hardly more than a recitation of a myth, or the consultation of an oracle, or the decoration of a grave, that the moods and motivations which sacred symbols induce in men and the general conceptions of the order of existence which they formulate for men, meet and reinforce one another. (See "Religion As a Cultural System," *The Anthropological Study of Religion,* edited by Michael Banton [The Association of Social Anthropology], Monograph Number 3, p. 28.)

What he is saying is that in ritual (or what we would call ordinances), our deepest motivations and deepest understandings merge. In all discussions of morality this, I take it, is the source of

BYU James E. Talmage Lecture, 1971.

power most often underestimated. And this is so even in our own midst. We need to recognize that ceremony is indispensable. And the most unanswerable evidence of the necessity of ceremony (notice I didn't say "desire" or "need," but a stronger word still —*necessity*) is that even those most hostile to it end by participation in it.

Look for a moment at worldly analogues. In student life, we see purportedly unstructured youth very structured indeed: the proper smudge on the shoes, the proper purr words (*neat, all right, swinging, grooving*), photographic imitation of rebuffs and greetings and departures, and even of the gesture that pushes the hair back. I am saying nothing against this; I'm not prescribing, only describing manifestations of symbolic gesturings—to show that there is no ceremonyless human being.

A friend of mine describes a laughable situation in which a group of men had banded together in a kind of social fraternal group. They all knew each other by first names and also in the Church by "brother." But they spent the evening in verbal stumbles, correcting themselves from "brother" to "worthy highmaster" and other such terms, trying to learn the new acceptable system.

The question then is not whether we will express ourselves in ceremonies. Inevitably we will. The question is, Which ceremonies are most powerful in motivating us in *becoming*?

The answer is, Those revealed from heaven.

Depth psychologists are telling us that touch, a handshake, the way we use space (to quote Edward Hall) has much to do with our balance in life. (You are only comfortable in conversation if the person is at a "proper" distance.) Scientist Polanyi speaks of the "tacit dimension" of life—what he calls "indwelling"—an intuitive, implicit consciousness of meaning which transcends "common sense," scientific method, or rational analyses; for example, recognizing (as we all do) the expression of puzzlement on a human face. There is Jung's notion of "the collective unconscious" which he elsewhere calls the great "symbol-making factory." He is convinced that each of us inherits not only our own parents' chromosomes but also a cumulative set of responses to symbolic forms.

Recognizing the power of symbolic ritual, many theologians today clamor for what they call a "liturgical revival." Protestants who whittled the seven sacraments to two (baptism and communion) and then decided they could get along with none at all now often wish they hadn't. They seek a new vital contact with the originals: "What did Jesus really do at the Last Supper?" "Would it help if we put a rock band in the St. John's Cathedral?" "Should there be a laying on of hands in confirmation?"

Semanticists today talk about how words often have roles or functions quite different than their dictionary meanings (for example, "I do" in a marriage ceremony). In their ritual functioning they take on something of the character of the thing they symbolize. C. S. Lewis alerts us to "semantic halos" and how they influence us beyond usual definitions. And J. L. Austin speaks of performatory utterances such as "I christen this ship," and "I baptize you," and describes these not as statements of fact but as ceremonial enactments—a doing of something through words. And he finds them immensely strong.

Formal mathematicians such as Tarski, Hempel, and Max Black have analyzed the nature of mathematics, which is the language of science, and have concluded that where mathematical definition is certain it has nothing to do with reality and when it is applied to reality it is misleading. Some acknowledge that personality, and especially religious expression, is not amenable to exact mathematical measure. And so (as a student of mine put it) the key to the universe may not be mathematics but metaphor, the language of compared qualities, the language of feeling. Ordinances are living metaphors or, as Orson F. Whitney put it, "poems in action."

The next step (to those of us who have not yet discovered this,

I offer it as a hypothesis) is to recognize that ordinances in the kingdom—from baptism to anointing to sealing—are the most intensively loaded and extensively applicable metaphors of the universe.

Let me pause here to warn against a certain hostility that I find in myself and assume may be in some of you. It arises not because we have correctly read the Restoration but because we have misread the Apostasy. We see remnants of ritual; we see them elaborated or embellished and also abandoned or reduced to things that are mystical or hollow or merely aesthetic. All of this we call "pagan ceremony." Thus, on guard against distortions, we are on edge about ordinances themselves. But when ordinances have been renewed, when their beauty has been revivified, when their appropriateness and significance has been reestablished, they are not pagan and they are not empty.

We turn then to two functions that ordinances can and ought to have in our daily lives.

It is Mircia Eliade, famous for his studies of the "symbolic structure" of religion, who says, "For the religious man, the cosmos lives and speaks." (*The Sacred and the Profane,* [New York City: Harper and Row, 1961], p. 165.) And he supposes that this is so because for *all* religions God or the gods have created the cosmos. But that, for Mormons, is a misstatement. Note two distinct propositions that stand behind our whole relationship to the earth and therefore to the ordinances:

First, the earth and the cosmos were not created. The elements are uncreate; the earth has been ordered, given form. The earth is not only the handiwork of God but it is somehow alive and is to be reverenced; the earth's destiny is to become a celestial body. The implication is that the earth is not to be escaped but transformed. And it pleases God that "the fulness of the earth is yours" and that "he hath given all these things unto man." (D&C 59:16.) It is not merely a bleak shadow of a higher world, it is on the way to *becoming* one.

Second, therefore, the distinction characteristic of all religion between sacred and secular—between what is holy and what is earthly—is finally artificial. We are taught, "All things unto me are spiritual." (D&C 29:34.)

Thus, modern revelation teems with assurance that every earthly human experience may be lived not only on a *higher* plane but eventually on the *highest*. Eternity is the extension—not the replacement—of the patterns of this earth.

Now, I suggest that ordinances as they have been reestablished in our midst are signs of reality, full-freighted with meaning. They are eternal teaching mechanisms. In confirmation, consider these three statements:

God has set many signs on the earth, as well as in the heavens; for instance, the oak of the forest, the fruit of the tree, the herb of the field, all bear a sign that seed hath been planted there; for it is a decree of the Lord that every tree, plant, and herb bearing seed should bring forth of its kind, and cannot come forth after any other law or principle." (Joseph Fielding Smith, comp., *Teachings of the Prophet Joseph Smith* [Salt Lake City: Deseret News Press, 1938], p. 198: hereafter cited as *TPJS*.)

In the Book of Moses the Master teaches Adam that "all things bear record of me." (Moses 6:63.)

And again, "All things which have been given of God from the beginning of the world, unto man, are the typifying of him." (2 Nephi 11:4.)

At the core, then, of all ordinances and all divinely revealed ceremonies are these signs of God and Christ which center in the source of life, the power of *becoming*. And this awareness with all its ceremonial enactments is the drive shaft of "consecrated" behavior.

Comparative religion tells us that many cultures have had rituals of fertility and their various offshoots: worship of the seasons, sun worship, the isolation of any and every kind of creature—scorpions, serpents, cows, and trees—to which are ascribed the powers of life, of generation, even of human regeneration. But these can and often do become idolatric. We are not to look *to* them but *through* them. They are signs of the ultimate source of life—Christ himself.

It is interesting to me that the word *ordinance* has the same root as *ordained* and *order*. Those connotations are appropriate. But it also has the same root as *ordinary*. That, too, is relevant. An ordinance takes the most ordinary of elements (for what is more commonplace than water, bread, olive oil?—kneeling, clasping hands, lifting of arms are ordinary things) and gives them or receives them or consecrates them as holy, as somehow focusing our mortal upreach and an immortal response. Ordinances make possible the transformation of the ordinary. Our ordinary work, ordinary breathing and speaking, ordinary pleasures, become extraordinary when they are consciously sacramental.

The later sermons of the Prophet Joseph Smith (who, until the Restoration, was taught that no sacrament is essential) abound with concern that the Saints understand this. One sees some frustration in him that the Saints—even they—are slow to understand. One statement, by the way, is itself a remarkable figure which time has blurred. He said getting this idea into the minds of the Saints was (here comes the simile) like "cutting hemlock knots using a corn-dodger for a wedge, and a pumpkin for a beetle." That is meaningless until you go back to his usage. Hemlock knots are tough to split, among the toughest. If your "wedge" were a cornmeal pancake and if the "hammer" with which you drove it in were a pumpkin you would know the difficulty of the task.

Some of Joseph's anxiety shows in a comment he made when the brethren were inquiring (after all, they had no precedent experience), "Why sacrifice to build the Kirtland Temple?" What did "endowment" mean anyway? The Prophet replied that he could not answer yet. "Nor could Gabriel explain it to the understanding of your dark minds." (*TPJS*, p. 91.) I'm afraid that means (and this is a frightening thought) that even God cannot explain fully until we open to him and his light.

But sparks of insight come out of the Prophet's teaching about ordinances, "that they may be perfect in the understanding of their ministry." (D&C 97:14.) Aren't there better ways of teaching than ordinances? "Who can I teach except my friends?" Plato asks. We can only learn some things in an environment of love—consecrated space and time—where we are approved and embraced. I'm a professional educator aware of lecturing, case method, class participation, summary, role playing, story, repetition, examination, personal reports, group dynamics, maps, audio-visual aids, dial access. Yet the kernel of worth of all of these is improved and enhanced by intelligent participation in ordinances. I wish we had another word for the blending of thought and feeling that takes place in an ordinance, a word perhaps like *compre-feel*. In modern thought, brain and heart are separated and often detached from the subtler aspirations of the spirit (sometimes the psychologists are responsible). But in ordinances, a symphonic combination of all aspects of the self occurs.

Again, the Prophet said ordinances combine the beautiful and the true. Those are my words, but listen to his. He is talking here about the ceremony for greeting one another to welcome them into the School of the Prophets. "I salute you in token or remembrance of the everlasting covenant." (D&C 88:133.) "Behold, this is beautiful that he may be an example." (D&C 88:130.) Again he tells us that ordinances are the triggering of memory—our infinite memories—for ordinances were established "from before the foundation of the world" and reveal things which have been "kept hid" until now. And we were there. Another scripture does not say that the Lord has given them for the first time, but that he has "renewed and confirmed" them. (D&C 84:48.) He does not say that we thus *begin* to share in his goodness here, but that we *"continue* in his goodness." The Prophet teaches further that these ordinances take away our facades, the many faces of Adam and Eve which we have constructed to mask our real selves. Face-to-face communion with God requires more than an arrival at a level where we can see his face. The problem is for us to decide which face to show him, which face is really authentic.

Some of you may be asking, "Can one develop a skill, an approach, a way of thinking that would help him understand more what is being taught in these rich signs and ordinances?" Here I am going to express a paradox.

On the one hand we sometimes need to leave behind logical, practical thought. There is a parallel here to the process of developing creativity, which has become the new universal value. (Nobody is against creativity today. But we know very little about it, especially about the "how" of it.) We know that it has something to do with the deeps, with spiritual respiration, with being on friendly terms with our subconscious, and that it flourishes best in an atmosphere of approval. (Nothing turns creativity off faster than for somebody to say, "Oh, no!" Then we wither.) In the same sense, I suggest we can open up to an even deeper than subconscious realm in us—the thirsting of the soul—and in silence that yields to Powers greater than our own, we can be filled.

On the other hand we need to remain practical. To me it is interesting that a man of great scholarly achievement (he had a Ph.D. in agrarian chemistry) found an answer to one of his chemical problems while in the temple. Paradox? I've just said, "Abandon the practical"; now I am saying, "Take your most worldly problems with you" into the ordinances. I quote him:

The endowment is so richly symbolic that only a fool would attempt to describe it. It is so packed full of revelations to those who exercise their strength to seek and see, that no human words can explain or make clear the possibilities that reside in the temple service.

What is true of the temple service is true of all the ordinances. Who am I quoting? John A. Widtsoe, the apostle. ("Temple Worship," *Utah Genealogical and Historical Magazine,* Vol. 12, pp. 55-64.)

There is something about ordinances that combines the universal and the particular. Not only are they tangible instruments of our own intimate spiritual need, they are themselves archetypal. Nothing about them is merely abstract in the old Platonic sense. Latter-day Saints know that we are closest to God when we are most personal, most intimately specific. Yet the whole thrust of western religion since Plato has been to glorify the abstract and even beyond that to introduce a premise of an utterly different order beyond this world which is both unknown and unknowable. Ordinances pull both worlds together for us until we come to know they are one.

Now the second great function. I've spoken of meaning and teaching, now I speak of power. Listen to these sentences:

In the ordinances thereof [and "thereof" refers back to the priesthood], the power of godliness is manifest. And without the ordinances thereof, and the authority of the priesthood, the power of godliness is not manifest unto men in the flesh." (D&C 84:20-21.)

A related statement: "Being born again, comes by the Spirit of God through ordinances." (*TPJS*, p. 162.) And another:

All men who become heirs of God and joint heirs with Jesus Christ will have to receive the fullness of the ordinances of his kingdom; and those who will not receive all the ordinances [and I interpolate "*all* that can be transmitted *through* the ordinances"] will come short of the fullness of that glory, if they do not lose the whole. (*TPJS*, p. 309.)

Our hesitancy to recognize ordinances as co-eternal with eternal principles is reflected here:

Ordinances instituted in the heavens before the foundation of the world . . . are not to be altered or changed. . . . There are a great many wise men and women too in our midst who are too wise to be taught. (*TPJS*, pp. 308-309.)

In the Doctrine and Covenants we are told we can discern "the spirits in all cases under the whole heavens" by one pattern or test—"if he obey mine ordinances . . . and . . . bring forth fruits of praise and wisdom." (See D&C 52:14-19.)

Somewhere George A. Smith, while Church Historian, described the difficulties the Prophet faced (in Kirtland) with the pre-Relief Society relief society. They hadn't yet organized. Some of the women received garbled accounts of what was taking place in the temple, and some were indignant, thinking it could only be mischievous. Elder Smith described how some members were disappointed that so little power was manifest in the temple and some were disappointed that so much—too much—was given. And this fine line between openness and receptivity and being closed was characteristic of our people then as it is now.

Ordinances in this setting are a form of prayer ("Ye receive the Spirit through prayer" [D&C 63:64])—perhaps the highest form. Krister Stendahl, one of the world authorities on the Book of Matthew, tells me it is conceivable that the Lord's prayer has been offered and sung these many centuries by millions with hardly a glimpse of its original intent. His study convinces him that the entire prayer was rooted in the expectation of the coming kingdom, therefore a new-making process. And for him, every sentence in it is to be translated into that invocation. Thus the phrase "Give us this day our daily bread," which I had supposed was a plea for physical survival, was really intended to say (according to Stendahl): "Give us today a foretaste, a sacramental touch with thee. Let us sit at table anticipating the day when we sit down together and partake of newness in thy presence."

Interestingly enough, such a sacrament meeting, when all worthies come together—all worthy—in the presence of the

Lamb, who is the "worthy-Maker," is promised in modern revelation—the revelation on the sacrament. It is taught that the sacrament is both a remembering and an anticipation. "For," says he, "the hour cometh that I will drink of the fruit of the vine with you on the earth. . . . And . . . with all those whom my Father hath given me." This is the preface of the later passages which I had never thought to connect to the sacrament of lifting up our hearts to rejoice, of girding our loins with truth, of taking on the whole armor of God, and of receiving what the Lord calls the "sword [sceptre] of my Spirit, which I will pour out upon you." This welding and wedding feast, of which Christ is the Bridegroom, is the preface to his final promise: "Ye shall be caught up, that where I am ye shall be also." (D&C 27.)

The language of Matthew and what I have cited from Doctrine and Covenants 27 is also clear in the omissions of 3 Nephi. Have you ever noticed that two phrases are there missing from the Lord's prayer as given in Matthew 6? They are "Thy kingdom come," and "Give us this day our daily bread." (3 Nephi 13:9-13.) Surely Joseph Smith, knowing the worldwide familiarity with this prayer, would not have omitted them without reason. May we assume that Christ omitted them among the Nephites— and for the best of all possible reasons: The kingdom had come; *he* was with them. They had received the initiatory ordinances in a splendor that imparted to them also the brilliant whiteness of the Savior. (3 Nephi 19:25.) The Beatitudes were not taught then as challenges to the will, a set of separate virtues; they came as a description of the tangible fruits that follow from receiving Christ, that he might baptize them all "with fire and the Holy Ghost." What we see in 3 Nephi (the phrase occurs "neither can it be written") is what Elder Talmage called "an ineffable outpouring of prayer." It was prayer that took them into the water and into the ordinances of fire, that led them to the touch of his very person and the healing of an entire multitude. That fire burned for four generations among a people (the Prophet Joseph later said) who were unusually persevering either in righteousness or in wickedness.

Did you know that the word *active* does not occur in the Doctrine and Covenants? The word *act* occurs fifteen times, but interestingly enough ten of these are verb forms: "acting in my name," "acting in concert," "acting in the office" to which one is appointed. If we need a word to describe a man who is admirable in the Lord's eyes the Doctrine and Covenants provides one: He is a "lively" member. One can be active and comparatively dead. But a lively member is something else. Alive! Elsewhere the book speaks of "plants of renown"—those who are planted "in a goodly land by a pure stream," and who bring forth "much precious fruit."

We speak in the Church of attending the sacrament table to renew our covenants. We should also speak of making covenants thus to receive Christ's renewal. We speak in the Church of being severed in other ways simply by dimming our own minds and refusing to care and reach. We should remember the comment of one of the Council of the Twelve who, after his excommunication and then rebaptism and laying on of hands, looked up and said, "Light, light after fourteen years of darkness." Without the ordinances, I submit, we often act without life, have friction without fire, motion without emotion, and forms without the power thereof.

Now a few implications. First, a word about drugs. "Yes," Al Capp said to hostile students, "the drugs expand consciousness just like the bomb expanded Hiroshima." The very anxiety to be "turned on" is but the distorted concern for godly power. The fever and fervor, which is not always selfish, to "blow one's mind" is often an attempt to escape the emptiness, the absurdity, the hell that fills all too many homes and hearts. Huston Smith, an expert on world religions, has argued that there is a common element of certain drug-trips and certain religious experiences. (He is not fully aware of what *we* mean by religious experiences.) But he adds that drugs do not freshen our faculties, do not expand creativity. You cannot get admission into Harvard Graduate School if you use drugs. Experience has proved that such students just can't hack it. Drugs don't produce a whole and happifying personality. Drugs can produce kicks, bruising and destructive kicks, but not persons. They are a backfiring shortcut.

Second (strange subject), demonology. The same concern for power is manifest in our time in a widespread new interest (and it is a religious interest) in the occult, in Satanism, in demonology and witchcraft. More Ouija boards were sold in this country last Christmas than games of Monopoly. Astrology and its variations are taking as much energy as church service. One in five believe there is "something to it." The history of religion is replete with invented rituals for exorcism to ward off, to protect from, to put down, the evil ones, but just as often to invoke them. We have no such set in Mormonism. The ordinances that bring you closer to God by that same process give you increased power over the adversary. Tampering with the occult can begin with idle curiosity. Then one develops a pathetic preoccupation with the works of darkness. People start out, in boredom, to scare themselves. All too soon they hear a real footfall in the darkened hall.

Third, a word about aesthetics. To me it is strange that traditional religion (I have in mind both Catholic and Protestant wings) in the West—setting out with the premise that there are two radically different orders, this world and an "utterly other" higher world—has concluded that any earthly art must be at most a feeble gesture toward the divine order. Yet Catholicism (predominantly) has been the greatest harbor of the master artists of the West. To stand until your neck hurts looking up at the Sistine Chapel ceiling is to be impressed with this gift. But the Catholic theologian must say: "No, these are not pictures of realities! They are at most analogies—the finite and material for the infinite and immaterial. Nothing there corresponds to Divine Reality."

In contrast, we have a doctrine of "immaculate perception." The senses are eternal. In fact, we define the soul as "spirit and body inseparably connected," or what President Joseph Fielding Smith delightfully calls "a fusion." That means that the seeable, touchable, hearable realm is forever. The senses will never be replaced; they will only be enhanced. And it follows that we, of all people, have a foundation for superb art, the expression of great insight in the tangible levels of reality available on this earth.

If we are suspicious of this, it is partly because we can see the futility of art for art's sake. But we should be open to art—for man's sake. That approach will again obliterate the ordinary distinctions between sacred and secular art. At root all music, all painting, all artful motion—even the art of conversation or baking a loaf of bread—can have an eternal significance. It is the individualizing of ordinances. "Nevertheless thy vows shall be offered up in righteousness on all days and at all times." (D&C 59:11.) We may infuse them with our own individual creative talents. If we are to acknowledge the hand of God in all things, an indispensable first step is to summon him into all *our* things. Intrinsic in the outlook of our forebears was the view that their lives sanctified the earth itself, increased the water, softened the climate, tempered the frost, and brought fruitfulness to what was barren. Today as we have moved toward the city we must attempt the new challenge of doing this with steel and glass and machines. Then we may realize how much power—even sacred power—our created environment exercises in and through our lives.

And now a final comment. There is much talk today about the "loss of community," about loneliness and isolation. There is a unifying power that derives from ordinances—unity within the self, unity among selves—that is available in no other way. Today the word *power* has become a chant often symbolizing, though not admittedly, a craving for divisive or dictatorial or destructive power. But we are taught that Christ yearned to gather the world "as a hen gathereth her chicks" (a beautiful figure). Third Nephi adds, "that I may nourish you." (3 Nephi 10:3.) He wants to gather us "to receive the ordinances of his house and the glories of his kingdom." (*TPJS*, p. 308.) You can only perform an ordinance *with* someone and in relationship to a higher Someone. (Otherwise your performance is not an ordinance but an imitation). As the Prophet looked back over his life (near its end), he said, "If a skillful mechanic, in taking a welding heat, uses borax, alum, etc., and succeeds in welding together iron or steel more perfectly than any other mechanic, is he not deserving of praise?" (*TPJS*, p. 313.) My answer is: He is. Christ, through his eternal ordinances, is the welding heat. "For the presence of the Lord shall be as the melting fire that burneth." (D&C 133:41.)

In summary, it is in ordinances that the power to *become* is generated. Morality is lifeless unless it , is rooted in Christ's ordinances—for they are rooted in him. This is where the truth is. This is where the life is. All substitutes are husks, if they are not also poison. It is tragic for any of us to starve to death. It is even more tragic to starve to death in the midst of plenty.

Power from Abrahamic Tests

I would like you to go for a moment to a place where President Hugh B. Brown and I were together—just he, his doctor, and I—in a valley known as Hebron, a place now beautifully fruitful and where tradition has it that there is a tomb to father Abraham. As we approached, I, the guide—but in need of guidance—asked, "What are the blessings of Abraham, Isaac, and Jacob?"

Elder Brown thought a moment and answered in one word, "Posterity." Then I almost burst out, "Why, then, was Abraham commanded to go to Mount Moriah and offer his only hope of posterity?"

It was clear that this man, nearly ninety, had thought and prayed and wept over that question before. He finally said, "Abraham needed to learn something about Abraham." That is my text this morning.

You are aware that the record speaks of the incredible promise that Abraham, after years of barrenness—which in some

Address given at BYU devotional, October 12, 1971.

ways to the Israelites was the greatest curse of life—would sire a son who would in turn sire sons and become the father of nations. This came about after Abraham had left a culture where human sacrifice was performed. Abraham was then counseled, and if that is too weak a word he was *commanded*, to take this miracle son up to the mount.

We often identify with Abraham; we sometimes think less about what that meant to Sarah, the mother, and to Isaac, the son. If we can trust the Apocrypha, there are three details that the present narrative omits. First, Isaac was not a mere boy. He was a youth, a stripling youth on the verge of manhood. Second, Abraham did not keep from him, finally, the commandment or the source of the commandment. But having made the heavy journey (how heavy!), he counseled with his son. Third, Isaac said in effect: "My father, if you alone had asked me to give my life for you, I would have been honored and would have given it. That both you and Jehovah ask only doubles my willingness." It was at Isaac's request that his arms were bound, lest involuntarily but spontaneously he should resist the sinking of the knife. Though many have assumed it to be so, only the Book of Mormon records a prophet's words saying that this was in "similitude of God and his Only Begotten Son." (Jacob 4:5.)

As we later ascended the mount traditionally known as Mount Moriah—it is just inside the east wall of Jerusalem—we remembered a statement of Brother Ellis Rasmussen of BYU: one can believe that it was to that same mount that another Son ascended. And this time there was no ram in the thicket.

Scholars are widely split over this account. At one extreme are those who say that it could not be, that it did not happen, that the account is an allegory; that we have here a description of the internal struggle that Abraham went through in trying to leave behind his boyhood training in human sacrifice; that God would not require such a thing. One man put it to me this way: "That is a terrible way to test a man. A loving God would not do it."

At the other extreme are those who have held that the story, if not true to history, is nevertheless true to life. However, they go further. They almost rejoice in the contradiction. They say this story illustrates that faith must do more than go beyond reason. Faith, if it is genuine, pulverizes reason. We must, as Kierkegaard puts it, be "crucified upon the paradox of the absurd."

My testimony is that both the rationalists and irrationalists have misread. For in modern times we have been taught that this story does not simply lie in our remote past but in our own individual future. As modern revelation states, we must be "chastened and tried, even as Abraham." (D&C 101:4.) Do you remember after that more than nine-hundred-mile march from Kirtland to Missouri—a march that from all mortal appearance was a failure, for it achieved nothing—someone came to Brigham Young and said. "What did you get out of that fiasco?" He replied, "Everything we went for—experience." He could say that because he had only within hours been with the Prophet Joseph in a meeting where the Prophet had declared in substance: "Brethren, some of you are angry with me because you did not fight in Missouri. But let me tell you God did not want you to fight. He wanted to develop a core of men 'who had offered their lives and who made as great a sacrifice as did Abraham.' Now God has found his leaders, and those of you who are called to positions who have not made that sacrifice will be required to make it hereafter." (Joseph Smith, *History of The Church of Jesus Christ of Latter-day Saints*, ed. B. H. Roberts [Salt Lake City: The Church of Jesus Christ of Latter-day Saints, 1932-51], Vol. 2, p. 182: hereafter cited as *HC*.)

There is the recorded testimony of Wilford Woodruff and John Taylor, who described the Kirtland Temple experience—an outpouring so rich that some of those present honestly believed that the Millennium had come, that the era of peace had been ushered in, so filled were they with the spirit of blessing and love. The Prophet arose in that setting and said: "Brethren, this is the

Lord that is with us, but trials lie ahead. Brethren [he was speaking now to the Twelve], God will feel after you, and he will wrench your very heartstrings. If you cannot stand it, you will not be fit for the kingdom of God." All too prophetic was that statement. Half of the original Council of Twelve later, as the Prophet put it, "lifted up the heel" against him and against Christ. Four others were at least temporarily disaffected. Only two, Brigham Young and Heber C. Kimball, did not buckle under the pressure, and they were tried, too.

Let us look at the implications for now. We live in a time when many are saying we need commitment, a total kind of commitment, a "risk-everything" kind of commitment. On that subject many contemporary writers are eloquent. But on the question, To what does one commit? vagueness and often vagaries are all that are offered. Someone asked me once, "What is the definition of a fanatic?" I answered in Santayana's phrase, "A fanatic is a person who doubles his speed when he has lost his direction." But what then is the name of a person who doubles and quadruples his effort when he has found his direction? That is commitment.

It is a mistake to suppose that Abraham acted in total ignorance—that his leap was a leap in the dark. If you consult the Inspired Version or even the King James, it is apparent that Abraham saw in vision the Son of Man (with a capital *M* meaning Man of Holiness, the Eternal Father). He saw him; he saw his day; and he rejoiced. (See Genesis 15:12; John 8:56.) He received promises and accepted them. He was told, as our Pearl of Great Price reminds us, that he stood, even before mortality, among the mighty, the noble, and the great; that he was one of them; that he was chosen (which is more than simply called) before he was born; and, therefore, that there lingered in him a residual power of response to Christ that came out mightily in the hour of need. (Abraham 3:22-24.)

We have been told that we are of Abraham. We are his children. We have been taught that those of us who have joined the Church by conversion are just as much so as those of us who are born under the covenant. (See D&C 84:33-34.) We have been taught that the spiritual process that is to occur within us is not just a matter of changing names. It is a process whereby the blood itself is somehow purged, purified, and we literally become the seed of Abraham. (*TPJS*, pp. 149-150.) But those who are Abraham's descendants must also bear the responsibility of Abraham. (D&C 132:30-32.)

We live in the time when everybody is willing to talk about rights—civil rights, other rights—and when it is rare to hear the words *duty* and *civil duty*. There never was a right, I submit, that did not have a corresponding duty. There never was a duty that did not also eventually entail a right.

We talk often as if the priesthood is solely a privilege. It is also a burden, and many who have lived long in this Church know there are times, sometimes lengthy times, when the priesthood is much duty and very little right.

This leads to the statement allegedly made by the quotable J. Golden Kimball. Someone asked him how he accounted for the call of a certain brother to a certain position. He is supposed to have replied, "The Lord must have called him; no one else would have thought of him."

Someone else was also complaining about how difficult it was to follow a certain leader. (You see, it is not just a matter of following the request to give a spectacular amount. What if you are called to give less than you can give? What if you are called not to be called? What if you are told only to wait for a decision and be patient?) In answer to this complaint, J. Golden, says the legend, replied, "Well, some of them are sent to lead us and some of them are sent to try us." After the laughter and delight of that statement passes, the truth of it becomes apparent. All of us are sent to lead and to try each other. And the priesthood is given to try us to the *core*.

May I speak only for a moment, out of the abstractions, about some modern examples. We have a historian who has recently been through eight hundred journals and diaries of our early forefathers. Two sentences leaped at me. One from John Pulsipher, who was on an Indian mission, reads, "A man can be happy in a cave if it is his duty to be there." The other is an entry in the diary of John Bushman. He was on the Little Colorado, where water was the source of all life and where irrigation was the critical survival factor. Again and again they would build a dam, and just as often he recorded that the dam broke. On one occasion he said only that the dam broke again, and recorded, "We are not discouraged." (Davis Bitton, *Guide to Mormon Diaries and Autobiographies* [Provo: BYU Press, 1977], pp. 51, 284.)

What about the Stegner article titled "Ordeal by Handcart"? You are aware that the Donner party, under the terror of their trauma, lapsed into cannibalism. Not so with these modern human yet superhuman Mormon saints. Some of them died in each other's arms. Some died with their hands frozen to the crossbar, always with their faces west.

Then there were the three young men—Brother Huntington, Brother Grant, Brother Kimball—all only eighteen years of age, who went with the relief party the "second thousand miles" to help the Martin handcart company. On this trip they faced a stream that was swollen with ice and snow. Have you ever walked, even to the knee level, through such water? The pioneers almost hopelessly stood back, unable to go through in their weakened and emaciated condition. Those three boys carried every one of the company across and then crossed back, sometimes in water up to their waists. All three later died from exposure. When Brother Brigham heard of their heroic act, he wept and then rose in the majesty of his spirit and said, "God will exalt those three young men in the celestial kingdom of God."

What about Brother Helaman Pratt, who had been in four states—driven from all—and who now had a toehold within an adobe house in the Salt Lake Valley. Brigham Young called him in and said: "Brother Pratt, we are calling you to colonize in Mexico. You will be released when you die. God bless you." Brother Pratt went. He was released when he died.

There are sacrifices. But the prophets again and again insist that we ought to use a different word. How can it be called a sacrifice to yield up a handful of dust when what is promised is a whole earth? But we think we know better than God. We think that what we want for us is greater than what he wants for us. Then we simply violate the first commandment, which is to love God first and over all. The moment that pattern is followed he seeks in us the one thing that we do not *really* want to give up. No, we do not respond. Many of us will say that we do not have that kind of faith. I submit to you that you do not have that kind of faith until you pass that test.

Now we are back to the statement, the wise statement, of Elder Brown: "Abraham needed to learn something about Abraham." What did he learn? He learned that he did love God unconditionally, that God could now bless him unconditionally. Do you think his prayers had a different temper and tone after that? Do you think he could pray in faith saying, "Lord, you know my heart," and the echo would say, "And *I* know it"? John Taylor said that the Prophet taught that if God could have found a deeper way to test Abraham he would have used that. (*Journal of Discourses*, 24:264.) As Paul looked back and wondered how Abraham could have his willingness account for righteousness, his conviction was that Abraham believed Jehovah could raise his son from the dead if necessary in order to fulfill the promise which that sacrifice scene contradicts. That is what God did ultimately with his own Son. (Hebrews 11:19.)

All about us there are quibblings, demeanings, oppositions, negations, shrinkings. But I, as one who has feet of clay that go all the way to my groin, bear my testimony this morning that it is the love of God that cries out for us to prove our love for him. He cannot bless us until we have been proved, cannot even pull out of us the giant spirit in us unless we let him. If we come offering what we think he wants, without having testimony that we are doing what he really does want, we are not yet prepared. I bear testimony that in the record there is also evidence that joy can attend us even in the midst of such sacrifice. It is a sweeter, perhaps a bitter, sweeter joy. But it comes when we know that we are acting under the will of Christ. There is also the testimony that when we thus respond he delights, he rejoices, with a power that is born of his own descent into pain.

Abraham was called the friend of God, the son of God, the father of the faithful. Modern revelation tells us that now he is a little higher than the angels. Abraham, says the revelation, sits with Isaac and Jacob on thrones, "because they did none other things than that which they were commanded." (D&C 132:37.) They are not angels but are gods and have entered into their exaltation.

May I make a personal reflection. Years ago, there was a moment when I became intoxicated with the idea that I could become a Rhodes Scholar. It did not take me long to become convinced that that was also what God wanted for me. The greatest shock of my life to that point was when, after passing certain of the preliminaries with the committee, I sat down and heard the committee announce two other names as going to Oxford. I was baffled. "You must be kidding," I thought. "Don't you understand? This is for me." But they did not make a mistake.

I remember giving a talk in a local ward the following Sunday—I am afraid a hypocritical talk—on prayer, where I announced that one of the great principles we had been taught is that when we pray we must always say, "Thy will be done," and then listen for it—that half of prayer was listening. As I said that,

I heard something, a kind of an imp on my shoulder saying: "You're a fine one to talk that way. You've been saying, 'Thy will be done as long as it's my will' for months. Now you're bitter, bitter as gall." Suddenly, without any introduction that the audience could have understood, I said, "I prophesy [strange thing for me to say, for I had never done that before] that the thing that I had expected and wanted but which has been denied this week will somehow be made up to me—that what I am to do (and I don't know what that is) will somehow be better than what I was to do." And then, quite confused at what I had heard, I sat down.

I forgot that completely until the time came when, in circumstances I cannot here relate, it became clear that I could do graduate studies at Harvard in New England. I had forgotten any relevance in that until the hour came (thirty-five years earlier than I had hoped) that I was called to be a missionary again, and a mission president in New England. I know there are those who will say: "You might just as well have gone to England and to Oxford, had you been able to cut the mustard. It is only a coincidence." I am here this morning to say that I am convinced in my soul that what was intended for me was not old England but New. When I prayed the bitterness out and the lingering peace of the Savior in, I had nothing but gratitude.

Today we need Abrahams, Isaacs, and Jacobs. We need those who are willing to stand and who, having done all, *stand*. We have people now, and need more, who can listen to the *living* word and the *present* commitment of the Lord Jesus Christ through his prophets and stand. May God help us to respond and become sons of Abraham.

Conscience
and Consciousness

Conscience is a will-o-the-wisp."

"Psychologists just don't credit conscience these days."

"*Conscience* is merely the name of moral rules we learned in childhood."

These three utterances, common among students of human behavior, are more or less widely believed today. And if behavioral scientists find traditional theories of conscience unreliable, slippery, and misleading, so do many analytic philosophers. There are variations on the theme, but the chorus maintains a kind of harmony: conscience or "moral sense" is reducible to the "no-no's" of one's childhood, a somewhat accidental collection of the mores and customs of those around us, the husk in which we grew. The conclusion that is often drawn is that we may safely—and even wisely—ignore these moralistic trappings. At least we must not take them too seriously.

Address prepared for the Commissioner's Lecture Series, Church Educational System, and delivered in 1973 at the LDS Institutes of Religion at Weber State College, Ricks College, and the Church College of Hawaii.

The purpose of this talk is to question both the premises and the conclusions of this outlook. And to recommend an inlook, a push toward origins that are adequate to the phenomenon of conscience, which, for me at least, is phenomenal. This is not, then, a defense of conscience but rather of the notion that at root it needs no defense.

But immediately an objection is raised: What is meant by *conscience*? Does not the word mean all things to all men? In the name of "conscience" has not every form of human behavior (for example, murder, theft, betrayal—and their opposites—and everything in between) been justified by men? And is there anything that has ever been praised that has not also been condemned by someone's conscience? And has not every theory of conscience been seriously opposed?

A beginning point is needed. Let me begin, then, with a seemingly uncritical and careless thesis, though I am convinced it is the best way to be critical and careful on the subject. That is to assume that all of us already have an awareness, indeed a haunting awareness, of what the word *conscience* signifies. Analytic definition would, if there were any need of it, be too late. To approach conscience without distorting it we must let it be, let it speak for itself, and in its own way. There may be need to remove semantic scales from our blurry eyes, but that is mainly because we have become adept at throwing dust. What is needed is less preoccupation with paralyzing definition and more with living introspection—with open, honest, uncluttered scrutiny of what is there below the layers of convention and cover-up. In the end, to demand a definition for conscience is analogous to demanding proof for one's own existence. In order to ask the question seriously, one must suppress the thing he demands.

If that analogy seems far-fetched, hear me out anyway.

Much discussion in the history of western ideas has focused less on what conscience is than on what it seems to say. And in response to this question, three main kinds of answers are given:

First, some maintain that conscience is a kind of rule-bank that prompts ethical and perhaps also legal and social maxims without applying them to specific cases. On this view what we "hear" when conscience speaks is such an imperative as, "You ought always to keep your promises," or, as W. D. Ross also insists, "You ought always to maximize the good." In the same line John Stuart Mill maintained that the idea of the greatest good of the greatest number—the principle of utility—is both given and assured by conscience.

A second view is that conscience is silent with respect to rules but takes situations or cases one by one. In the actual, practical, work-a-day world, conscience tells a man what is and what is not appropriate behavior. Often this caution is cast in negative terms. Socrates, for example, claimed that his inner voice or "daemon" warned him of the wrong course of action but did not speak on the right. On this view one cannot arrive at guiding principles through his conscience. Conscience only speaks to one when he is in the real—or in some cases the imaginatively confronted—world of decision and conduct.

A third view is that conscience offers neither rules nor concrete guidance. Conscience is rather the measure of ideal persons. On this view we have a kind of moral sense or intuition by which we can recognize, admire, and seek to emulate the qualities of character or goodness in other men—conscience is a kind of hero-chooser after whom our life may be modeled. It is in this form conceived as a "guide" only in the sense that it provides ideal types of personal worth.

In my judgment all three of these views have hold of something authentic. But such accounts only magnify the intriguing question of origins. How came such remarkable insights; how explain their binding power even, it seems, in those who deny them binding power? In the final reckoning, does it make much sense to say that such perceptions and judgments are merely childhood "no-no's"?[1]

---

[1] I have nothing against childhood "no-no's." Many of them were, and remain, profoundly wise.

So much for a start.

Let us try now to come closer to the world of conscience itself,
our own data. And let us question at the outset the stereotype that
seems to dominate much of our common sense and conversation.

On this popular notion conscience is a combination policeman,
judge, and prison warden. When we run afoul of a rule or
commit an impropriety, conscience summons us to judgment—
always after the fact—always in retrospect. We are hauled into
court, and swinging a gavel that echoes in our spongy doubts and
fears, the judge says, "Guilty, guilty, guilty!" Thus one finds it
plausible to identify conscience with arbitrary parents, unkind
peer group members, and authority figures in general. Anything
to put the problem "out there" where we can do some arresting,
summoning, and sentencing of our own.

But clearly it isn't "out there." And, whatever our motives,
even a little self-scrutiny will show how much this portrait misses.

What is offered here as a nudge toward such scrutiny is
personal, subjective and, many will say, whimsical. But if
conscience does indeed speak and behave in any of these ways,
then to find out you need simply close your eyes and sweep
inwardly. For me there are elements here that are, introspectively
speaking, irrefutable, however clumsy the formulation.

But my case does not depend on total agreement of details. It
depends only on the acknowledgment that conscience is more
than the "nothing but" of the theories.

How *much* more is the question.

To begin with, there is something uncanny in the fact that
conscience not only judges in retrospect but in prospect. Long
before action or even deliberation it throbs its commendation or
withdraws it. Technically, each of our moral dilemmas, like every
event of life, is unique. Such change and relativity is often urged
against the validity of conscience or of any moral system. After all,

we ourselves are changing physically, mentally, emotionally; the
world environment is changing; institutions and laws are
changing. Conclusion? Conscience is outgrown, outmoded,
outflanked.[2] Yet conscience seems to me to cross all bridges
before we come to them—and even to challenge the profession of
bridge building. It seems both up-to-date and ahead of itself. In
the long run does it not shed our more foolish misreadings and,
regardless of change, refuse to be silent?

Then again, the stereotype misses the positive ring of
conscience. Our language contains many conscience words that
are negative in connotation: *uneasiness, twinge, bother, pang, smiting,
gnawing, fever,* and the like. We even say, "My conscience is killing
me."[3] Yet there is such a thing as a "clear conscience," and from
the same source, it seems, there come purrings, approvals,
rejoicings, and, as it were, songs of peace. Does not conscience kiss
as well as bite?

Third, conscience is concerned with more than acts. One of its
amazing but also maddening traits is that it just won't keep its
nose out of anything. It takes on our motives, our thoughts, our
feelings, our attitudes, including our motives, thoughts, feelings,

---

[2]From the Stoics to Aquinas there have been attempts to construct a theory of "natural
law"—a law of human nature—which is unequivocal and exceptionless; and to derive absolute
moral judgments from it. This speech is not intended to resolve that issue. My own guess is that
the phenomenon of conscience—what Kant called "the moral law within"—has given the theory
of natural law whatever plausibility it has enjoyed. But the power of conscience to change, to
grow, and to become increasingly intense and to adapt to novel circumstances gives it a special
role which no finite formulation of exceptionless law can do. Moreover, it is conscience, or
something closely related to it, that helps us past the conflicts that arise between fixed
obligations; for example, the promise to lend a gun, and, in the meanwhile, the recognition
that the borrower intends to use it to commit a crime. "Natural Law" theories always lead to such
conflicts. Only by maintaining that man has only *one* obligation to which all other considerations
are to be subserved, can they avoid the clash of competing principles. And no theory that I know
of has ever made good the claim to a "one only" obligation.
Mormonism is pluralistic in its obligation-claims. And therefore, it acknowledges the
constant possibility of conflict. These can only finally be resolved by a higher, present, and living
decision. It follows that Mormonism can never be reduced to a set of moral laws—even to the
proclamation of eternal and unchanging laws. Its essence requires indispensable living
adaptation to changing circumstance: living prophets, not simply rule books; living conscience,
not simply habitual discipline; and above all a living Christ, who speaks to the present, not simply
a set of sentences spoken about him, or even by him, in the past.

[3]Of course, it is not conscience but the violation of it that does the killing. The wages of sin,
not conscience, is death.

and attitudes toward it. It is fussy and finicky enough to strain at a gnat; for example, the slight edge of voice I let slip into a sentence spoken to a child. But it also claims vast and presiding awareness of the sort of person I may be way down the road, and it tells me to get on with it.

That leads to its reflexive, whole-self character. A policeman, a judge, a warden enter our lives and claim authority over us for a specified time. But conscience claims authority over us all the time. And not only the actual us, but the potential us, that much-smothered and momentous self that is somewhere beyond our present achievement or reach. At this level, conscience is a kind of rider with spurs, sometimes gently, sometimes ruthlessly, prodding. Parents are often taught to judge and reprove a part of a child, his hand or his mouth or his present temper tantrum. But conscience, if I mistake not, has no such scruples. It holds one accountable for himself—all of himself. It acknowledges conditioning and extenuating circumstances and forgives you when you really can't help or hinder certain forces. But it insists you are a cause—*the* cause—of the way you respond to the bombardment. Conscience can *never* be converted to fatalism or determinism.

For this reason it is superficial to identify conscience and guilt. Even in the person comparatively guilt-free, conscience is at work sponsoring projects and related concerns. One is given only so much rope and time to celebrate any particular achievement (and if it is an easy thing, less than one is capable of, no time at all) before there begins a buildup of inner striving which eventually reaches concert pitch: "Become more!" If this is so, it unmasks the cliché which suggests that conscience surfaces only when we are facing crises or imminent death, at which point "our whole life goes before us." There is indeed—who of us does not know it—a fantastic compounding of consciousness in that split second when we fall overboard or hear a screech just before a crash on the freeway. It is a stark regaining of what one thought he had forgotten. ("What will my mother think?" said a Chicago gangland youth as he fell to the pavement after a fatal stabbing.) But is conscience ever so tardy? To our reproach or defense, "Why didn't you tell me sooner?" doesn't it say, "I did!" or more precisely, "I always have!" or more precisely still, "I am the you you've been hiding from!"? One can hide only from what he knows—or at least suspects—is there.

Nor is guilt always a negative. And here we approach one of the paradoxes of conscience. The very intensity of one's guilt about his life and himself is double-edged. On the one hand it tells him something is wrong; and the more terrible the guilt, the more terrible the wrong. But it is not only diagnosis, it is also therapy. For it tells him that something is marvelously right; that something within him—I repeat, *within* him—cannot be muffled or denied. In which case, the guiltier he is, the more worthy, sensitive, and enlightened. If there were not this better-judging self, guilt could not occur. Pigs, one writer has observed, do not have psychoses; chickens do not hang their heads in shame. Man is distinguished from other entities, animate or inanimate, in his capacity for the fever of unresolved guilt. And conscience is clear on *how* to resolve it. How powerful this can become and how utterly independent it often is of conventional ethnic or social mores can be shown in some extreme cases.

It is reported, for example, that in some prison camps in Vietnam and elsewhere, sadistic guards have continued their grisly and vicious careers for years—then, one day, they have thrown down their steel whips, screaming: "I can't do it! I can't do it!" Why not?

In the same manner, some psychotherapists allege that regardless of how deranged or hallucinatory a person may be, one touch with reality remains with startling clarity. It is the recognition of the genuine as distinct from the pretended concern of the doctor or nurse. In other words, even the sickest of men recognize a deceitful personality from a genuine and loving one. One wonders if, similarly, they recognize these distinctions inside themselves.

And then there are "incorrigible" murderers on death row. If we can trust Capote's interviews, they have a remarkable pattern in common. Most prisoners can recall details of the events preceding their violence, but at the point where the actual crime began they "blank." They say, over and over, that they cannot believe they were actually there. It was "someone else" or, they insist, they were "not themselves." This apparently is more than the legal resort of temporary insanity. It is the insistence that they cannot recall responsible action. The forgetfulness is analogous to the tendency of our memories to refuse us recollection of deep horror or trauma. But if the criminal is "hardened," why should his murder be traumatic? Do we have here a failure of conscience or a witness of its power? Nietzsche summed it up shrewdly: " 'I did that,' says my memory. 'I could not have done that,' says my conscience. Eventually the memory yields."[4]

Again, the stress we often place on guilt and on fear leaves out of the picture another element of conscience—its promising power. It not only commends and commands a way of life for us but also promises fulfillment. Far from being a tartan that knows only the language of duty, responsibility, and sacrifice, does not conscience speak eloquently about satisfaction, completion, gratification, and even glorification; and how mean and trivial we are to postpone them? Hamlet observed correctly that a troubled conscience may make cowards of us all. But so it may make dynamos. Reinhold Niebuhr once listened to a committee who were ambivalent about accepting Rockefeller's endowment of the New York Center for Columbia University. "He didn't do it because he believes in education," they said, "but because of a guilty conscience." Niebuhr replied, "What's wrong with a guilty conscience?" Indeed, what is? Conscience reenthrones our neglected hold on the things that matter most.

Implicit in all this is what conscience seems to imply, in fact, to

---

[4]But not completely. For we shall have "a perfect knowledge of all our guilt . . . and the righteous shall have a perfect knowledge of their enjoyment." (2 Nephi 9:14; compare Alma 11:43.)

presuppose about itself. It seems completely at home with infinity, with time and space, with truth and beauty. It presupposes a whole cosmology and psychology—both what I really do want and what I really ought to want; and more amazing—how they may one day converge. Its horizon is never limited to present preoccupations. Perhaps this is why Heidegger is so impressed that conscience is all the time reminding us that time is passing and pleading that we act under the sense of the totality—the farthest limit being death. And whether conscience is equally insistent on its own indestructibility and mine—it seems to assume that here is something I cannot outsmart, outgrow, outlive, or outdie. Future reckoning is inescapable.

Everything for future reference, it seems—but also for future reverence. And now appears the most remarkable thing of all, which perhaps only the religious-minded will follow. How many times do we have to tell conscience—in how many situations—"This has nothing to do with God." Remorselessly it urges the contrary, "It has everything to do with God." The message recurrent, and somehow strangely reminiscent—against which I for one have never been able to provide insulation—is that every deliberate wrong or shoddy performance of mine is a form of blasphemy, that sin is ingratitude, that every abuse of my potential—and of others'—is a concession to ugliness and a hurt to the Divine. In short, conscience generates in me (and in so many of those I talk to) a permeating sense of the sacred. And in its resistance to darkness and its insistence on light, one would think at times it is almost omniscient.

A phenomenal phenomenon, then. Will you grant me that much? How to explain it?

Carl Jung takes a step toward adequacy. After several decades with patients in consulting rooms, he theorized that you and I have access to much, much more than has been written on us during our singular lifetime. Somehow, by the mysteries of inheritance, we possess, he claims, a racial memory. Below, as it were, our own individual subconscious, there is the "collective unconscious," a treasure-house of experience which undergirds our cognitive gropings and affects every impulse and judgment. Jung's interpreters have sometimes called this a "symbol-making factory," for it even conditions our selections of word usage and our preferences for symbolic expression—our desire, for example, to close an unfinished circle or to add a note to a musical phrase. This realm, Jung concluded, is properly called "religious." And for him the source of much human maladjustment is failure to give it proper sway in our lives.

So we can theorize that the race is somehow in us. But then how do we account for what, seemingly from the earliest traceable outset, is in the race? The question takes us a step further and puts meaning in four breathtaking sentences of modern revelation:

Man was also in the beginning with God. . . .

Behold, here is the agency of man, and here is the condemnation of man; because that which was from the beginning is plainly manifest unto them, and they receive not the light.

And every man whose spirit receiveth not the light is under condemnation.

For man is spirit. (D&C 93:29, 31-33.)

Only something of such magnitude, I submit, can account for the full phenomenon and power of conscience. What is "plainly manifest" to us, which is to say, within us, is an intimate and infinite relationship. This implies that in God's environment, but also in ours, there was conscious, vital, personal nurture through epochs that can be measured only in light years. And though presently a veil is drawn over specific images of that realm—we do not now recall our name, rank, and serial number—there is built in us and not quite hidden a "collective unconscious" that is superracial in character, a pool of such vivid effect, such residual power in us, that our finite learnings and recoveries are at best a tiny aftermath. "Man is spirit"—this spirit. And it breathes in us with a cumulative, crystal consciousness.

Thus opens up a whole new dimension of awareness and responsibility. Conscience at this level may be subsumed under law—for what we are derived from is the essence of what we are akin to. As a candle flame leaps to another candle flame or as a stream finds a river, so "intelligence cleaveth unto intelligence," says the revelation. And likewise "wisdom receiveth wisdom"; "truth embraceth truth"; virtue loves virtue; light, light; and mercy, mercy. (D&C 88:40.) There are matching antipathies to deception, to hate, to vice, to unforgiving domination. Clearly conscience and the light which is in us and which comes afresh from God and his Christ are not identical. Yet one is the record or testimony of the other and all, as the revelation says, "plainly manifest." (D&C 93:31.) How plainly and how manifest will differ for each of us as we give full expression to our hidden possibilities. But the Prophet Joseph once suggested how the impress is nonsensuous, "given," he said, "as though we had no bodies at all"[5]—and yet so persistently sensible. If it is short of perfect knowledge it is nevertheless the knowledge of perfecting. It is that cluster of assurances that linger in us like the warming impressions of a departed friend, giving thirst and thrust toward reunion.

One implication of all this can now be put in the form of an imperative: Give your conscience its way—protect, cherish and measure it with the light—and you will eventually see the hand and handiwork of God and goodness everywhere, most of all in yourself. Flout, abuse, betray, repress it, and you will eventually see his hand nowhere, not even in yourself. That is how moral conscience and religious consciousness interact and become one.

The two processes are vividly at work in a man who is thoroughly contemporary, though he lived seventy-four years before Christ. He

---

[5]All things whatsoever God in his infinite wisdom has seen fit and proper to reveal to us, while we are dwelling in mortality, in regard to our mortal bodies are revealed to us in the abstract, and independent of affinity of this mortal tabernacle, but are revealed to our spirits precisely as though we had no bodies at all." (*TPJS*, p. 355.)

is all the more persuasive because he really has a purchase, in each of his arguments and protests, on the truth. Sometimes what he affirms is true, but what he denies false. Sometimes he pushes his affirmations and denials to irrelevant extremes. But he is no strawman. Nor is he shut up safely within the thirtieth chapter of Alma. He and his arguments are in all of us. So much so that I am giving them fashionable contemporary labels. They come along, as the high priest said Korihor came along, to "interrupt our rejoicings." (Alma 30:22.) Look at the nine-point conscience-cover he advocates.

First, positivism, the insistence on the senses. "Ye cannot know of things which ye do not see." (Alma 30:15.) This is splendid methodology for science, though even scientists with their precise instruments cannot "see" electrons. In contrast, one must often close one's eyes in order to "see" his conscience. Of course, by one definition one cannot "see" one's past, one's guilt, nor the pain (or peace) of conscience. It does not follow that he cannot know them. Will we not acknowledge that sometimes night pillows know more of our depths than the noonday sun because that is when we are left alone without the balm of distracting objects? "But," persists the argument, "only an infinite series of observations could tell us for sure that this mass of data is not illusory." To which one answer is that an infinite series is what we have already had and are already responsible for.

Second, psychologism. Conscience is not "objective." "Behold, it is the effect of a frenzied mind." (Alma 30:16.) The question may be asked, Who is more frenzied, one who honors conscience or one who abdicates it? Frenzy can give fuel to disbeliefs as well as to beliefs. And it is protective discoloration to hold that all who condemn us or approve us, including our unoriginated inner voice, are "sick, sick, sick." In truth, the outcry of conscience may, for the moment, be the only healthy thing left in us.

Third, environmentalism. "It's just a matter of custom." "And this derangement of your minds comes because of the traditions of your fathers, which lead you away into a belief of things which are not so." (Alma 30:16.) By using antiquity as a club and modernity as ploy, Korihor conceals the antiquity (eternality?) of his own position. Conscience knows that neither is to the point. Wisdom does not become folly the moment we call it "tradition," or "the establishment," or the "local provincialism." How often, for example, we ask, "Were you born into your religion?" "Yes." "Uh huh!" we reply, as if that explains everything. The assumption is that one can no more choose his religion than he can choose his parents. But what if, in the light of spirit-sweeping vision we embraced and now reembrace both? It is often said that if you had been born to someone else you would have a different set of values, a different potential. Perhaps so. If only we hadn't been born of God.

Fourth, the power-ethic, the argument of self-sufficiency. "There [can] be no atonement made for the sins of men, but every man fare[s] in this life according to the management of the creature; therefore every man prosper[s] according to his genius, and . . . every man conquer[s] according to his strength." (Alma 30:17.) Shades of Darwin and Nietzsche. And a bright half-truth—the fittest *do* survive. In what sense was Christ "fit" and in what senses did he survive? True religion expands life-power until it matches that of God himself, which is the only genuine and final survival. His power is always used to expand, not exploit, his creatures. But power over one's enslaved and enslaving weaknesses and over all the varieties of death and all the consequences of our acts requires help. And no one can, in good conscience, deny his need of help. We argue incessantly over which is the more important, Christ's influence or our own. That is a strange pastime when in truth both are indispensable. But, worlds without end, Christ cannot help us until we let him. Isn't that what conscience says?

Fifth, relativism and nihilism. Anything goes, and anyway it all comes to nothing. "Whatsoever a man [does is] no crime." (Alma 30:17.) "When a man [is] dead, that [is] the end thereof." (Alma 30:18.) The ancient death wish. "Who can say what is right or wrong?" The nerve of the argument is, again, irrelevant. What comfort can I gain from learning that people who reinforce conscience are gone or that other people want other things? And why assume that conscience would be reliable only if it said exactly the same thing to everyone? It does not follow logically. We try to make it follow psychologically. But it won't be forced. The extreme of this position, often held today, is that we ourselves create all the reality and all the meaning there is. But the argument so often begins and ends in despair. Conscience will tell you that reality is neither that flexible nor that ignorable.

Sixth, the freedom argument. "They durst not look up with boldness, . . . they durst not enjoy their rights and privileges." (Alma 30:27.) "Why do ye yoke yourselves with such foolish things?" (Alma 30:13.) "Behold, I say that a child is not guilty because of its parents." (Alma 30:25.) The edge of this protest is sharp and at times deserved. There *is* pseudo-guilt as there is also pseudo-forgiveness. And how often the churches have merchandised by creating the very guilt they claim to relieve. ("You are utterly depraved, therefore guilty.") And how many moderns have profited by saying for a large fee the reverse. ("Your guilt is only a product of infantile trauma and not genuine at all.") Each assists us to adjust to our sicknesses instead of healing them. In the long run conscience will not stand for either of these inducements. How redeeming the revealed insight—a doctrine of original righteousness—"every spirit of man was innocent in the beginning." (D&C 93:38.)

As for the "yoke," some (said a recent counselor) "will absolutely destroy themselves to prove they have a right to do it." But whom besides themselves are they trying to convince? Are they that much beholden to others? How constant our will to misunderstand the "bounds and conditions" of law and to oppose freedom to law! Law does not tell us what we *must* do. It tells us the inevitable consequences of what we *choose* to do. Conscience adapts and applies law. It does not—and cannot—destroy it. And only when we seek to vindicate conscience do we dare "look up" to God with a boldness based on revelation—the revelation of ourselves—rather than with the many faces of deception. Korihor, you remember, was "causing them to lift up their heads in their wickedness." (Alma 30:18.)

Seventh, antiritualism. Korihor attacks "the foolish ordinances and performances which are laid down by ancient priests, to usurp power and authority over them, to keep them in ignorance, that they may not lift up their heads." (Alma 30:23.) Sometimes true; but how shabby and circular the stance. Sin creates an antipathy to life, especially spiritual life. Then we stay away from the banquet because we have deeply betrayed the host. (Atheists don't find God for the same reason thieves don't find policemen.) We eat husks instead and then claim that the husks are the only food. It takes a little boy, like conscience, to observe that, just as the emperor had no clothes, we have no food. And it shows. The sacramental approach to life and the life-giving power of ordinances and sacraments are apparent to all who attend the banquet. We may indeed partake foolishly. But not to partake is worse than foolish. It is death.

Eighth, the hypocrisy charge. Sooner or later, but usually sooner, things get personal—and so does Korihor. "According to your own desires; and ye keep them down, even as it were in bondage, that ye may glut yourselves with the labors of their hands. . . . lest they should offend their priests." (Alma 30:27, 28.) Here is another irrelevant half-truth. No word comes more frequently to our lips in self-defense than "hypocrite." And how we straitjacket the word so its arms cannot touch us. Brought to its full fighting weight, our charge would mean that no one has the right to recommend or to rebuke a way of life unless he himself has achieved (or avoided) it. That would bind and also gag just about everyone— except Christ. Does anyone else need "room to talk"—to underwrite our conscience? As to the rest of us, supposedly smitten to silence, what a strange restriction. Really, now! A drunkard who has paid through the nose for what he imbibes through his mouth is now told he can salvage honor and credibility only if he shuts both! But no one on earth is more entitled to speak against alcoholism than the victim thereof; more, not less, when he is hopelessly addicted. If we could prove (to whom?) that the world, and especially our most vocal leaders, are full of hypocrisy, what then? The compulsive hope that we can get off the hook by tarring them with the same brush is itself hypocritical in the self-deceptive (not just other-deceptive) way Christ exposes.

Ninth, atheism masked as agnosticism. "By their traditions and their dreams and their whims and their visions and their pretended mysteries . . . they . . . offend some unknown being who they say is God. . . ." (Alma 30:28.) "I do not deny the existence of a God, but I do not believe that there is a God." (Alma 30:48.) This is an intellectual cover for the blind faith of militant atheism. An unknown God has the same advantage as a nonexistent one; neither can get in your hair. We may hammer at others, "Do not say you know when you don't." That may bury alive the whisper of our own conscience saying, "Do not say you don't know when you do." Earlier Korihor has shown us the extent of his rejection. "God—a being who never has been seen or known, who never was nor ever will be." (Alma 30:28.) This is not agnosticism but dogmatism, a vast negative faith. And shortly he claims to propose the acid test. "I will believe only if I see a sign."

The request is doubly dishonest, first because he would accept no sign as convincing, and second because he had seen signs. "Thou hast had signs enough," Alma replies. And so have we all. How many times must a man suffer before he admits that pain hurts? Why do we go on acting as if nothing up to this moment counts as evidence for God when we have been illumined innumerable times? To the man who finally cooperates with conscience (and Alma had earlier suffered in sin until his guilt led him to wish for extinction), "all things denote there is a God." (Alma 30:44.) To the man who shouts it down, nothing does. But now comes Korihor's admission, the pathetic confession, the acknowledged contradiction.

Korihor pours out his story. He has been a rebel with a cause. He has had his own kind of dream, whim, and vision. And did he ever suspect who was giving him his orders? "Go and reclaim this people," he was told by the very voice of an angel. "They have all gone astray after an unknown God." (Alma 30:53.) And why were such words so overpowering and why did he obey them? "Because they were pleasing unto the carnal mind." (Alma 30:53.) But how did he arrange to argue away the spiritual-minded impulses in himself? "I had much success, insomuch that I verily believed that they [his denials] were true." Thus strangely he accepted his followers' word as more valid than his own. Now he acknowledges that in the very midst of his campaign of disparagement, "I also knew that there was a God." Even this admission diminishes the scope of his knowing, for Alma's inspired words to him—"I know that thou believest"—demonstrate that Korihor could truthfully have acknowledged, "I *always* knew that there was a God." (Alma 30:52.) Always? Even when, as he says, he "verily believed" that his denials were true? Yes. But isn't that a contradiction? Yes. A more than logical self-contradiction into which all of us frequently fall. "And now when he had said this, he besought that Alma should pray unto God, that the curse might be taken from him." (Alma 30:54.) His objections were swept away—the truths, even the profound truths he mixed with his distortions, now useless in giving him relief or justification. In their place came the agonized cry for help, and the self-condemning[6] request that Alma do the praying.

Is conscience, then, a will-o-the-wisp, something to grow out of? I have offered a portrait that seems to me to render that sort of "explanation" an inadequate "explaining away" and to suggest instead that conscience at its best is something to grow into. In addition, I have illustrated how conscience, when flouted, diminishes consciousness; as, when honored, it invincibly expands it.

---

[6]"A man is his own tormenter and condemner," said the Prophet Joseph Smith. "Hence the saying, They shall go away into the lake that burns with fire and brimstone. The torment of disappointment in the mind of man is as exquisite as a lake of burning with fire and brimstone. I say, so is the torment of man." (*TPJS*, p. 357.)

Neither our ill-willed parodies of conscience nor the highly sophisticated rejection of ideas which we suppose will destroy it work out. In the best and the worst of us it is still there. It is one of the things—dare we put it so strongly?—that we cannot, here or hereafter, disbelieve. At its most illumined it becomes the will of the god within us, and the god of the will to become.

But how can anyone know without knowing he knows?

Just so. How can he?

The Intimate Touch of Prayer

Many have asked in my hearing: "How is it that the Prophet Joseph Smith, age fourteen, could go into a grove, never having prayed vocally (implying that he *had* prayed before in silence), and in that first prayer receive such great and marvelous blessings? Does that mean that he simply had far greater faith and worthiness than any of the rest of us?"

One response is that the visitations received by the Prophet Joseph Smith weren't an answer just to his own prayer, but to the prayers of literally millions, maybe even those beyond the veil, who had been seeking and reaching for generations for the restoration of the gospel—fulfillment, in fact, of a phrase offered by billions, "Thy kingdom come." (Matthew 6:10.) That is an important insight. You and I pray not alone. We pray as part of a great modern movement and are empowered in that very process. If we care—or even care enough to try to care—to be instruments, unique privileges descend upon us, among them the authorities and gifts and blessings of the Holy Ghost and the crowning blessings of the priesthood.

Based on an address given at the Know Your Religion Series, California, 1972-73; as published in the Ensign, *January 1976.*

The hallmark of the prayer-life of Joseph Smith is intimacy. "He told the brethren that was the kind of faith they needed—the faith of a little child going in humility to its parent, and asking for the desire of its heart." (Orson F. Whitney, *Life of Heber C. Kimball* [Salt Lake City: Bookcraft, 1973], pp. 69-70.) Many suppose it compliments God to speak of him and to him as "far off," utterly different, utterly transcendent. Their image of God, if they have an image, is of a fine high principle or "pure mind" or undifferentiated light. To Joseph, the first principle of religion (and also the first principle of prayer) is to know for a certainty the fatherly character of God—not only that God has a personal relationship with us, and we with him, but that God is a *person*, the highest and most complete person—and that we may converse with him just as Moses did, "as one man converses with another." Here is an instance recorded by Daniel Tyler when the Prophet exhibited such closeness:

I had heard men and women pray—especially the former—from the most ignorant, both as to letters and intellect, to the most learned and eloquent, but never until then [listening to the Prophet Joseph pray] had I heard a man address his Maker as though He was present listening as a kind father would listen to the sorrows of a dutiful child. Joseph was at that time unlearned, but that prayer, which was to a considerable extent in behalf of those who accused him of having gone astray and fallen into sin, that the Lord would forgive them and open their eyes that they might see aright—that prayer, I say, to my humble mind, partook of the learning and eloquence of heaven. There was no ostentation, no raising of the voice as by enthusiasm, but a plain conversational tone, as a man would address a present friend. It appeared to me as though, in case the veil were taken away, I could see the Lord standing facing His humblest of all servants I had ever seen. ("Recollections of Daniel Tyler," *Juvenile Instructor*, 27:127.)

Now let us ask some elementary questions about the Prophet's prayers to see how his experiences may overlap, but also intensify, our own.

Were his prayers brief or lengthy? A convert to the Church, Mary Elizabeth Rollins Lightner, then only fourteen years of age, describes coming with her mother to the Prophet's home and hearing a glorious sermon when the Prophet's countenance fairly shone and he testified of the nearness of Christ. Then Joseph asked that all present kneel, and he prayed. She recalls: "I have never heard anything like it since. I felt he was talking to the Lord and the power rested upon us all. The prayer was so long that some of the people got up and rested, then knelt again." (*Diary of Elizabeth R. Lightner,* BYU Special Collections, p. 3.)

On the other hand, one day at home in Kirtland when there was precious little food on the table, he stood and said: "O Lord, we thank thee for this johnny-cake and ask thee to send us something better. Amen." Shortly, a knock sounded at the door and there stood a man with a ham and some flour. The Prophet rejoiced: "You see, Emma. I knew the Lord would answer my prayer." (*Juvenile Instructor,* 27:172.) That was a telegram prayer, not a long letter.

The long and short of it is that some prayers should be long and some short.

Did the Prophet address the Lord as "Father," or did he have a special manner or title of address? Most frequently he prayed "our Father," or simply "Father" or "O Lord," and was not inclined to embellish that title with adjectives and flowery phrases. Such adjectives may be appropriate, but for him the simple "Father" was sufficient. And in that, as in so many ways, his prayers were akin to the prayer patterns of Christ himself.

He said on occasion, "Be plain and simple and ask for what you want, just like you would go to a neighbor and say 'I want to borrow a horse and go to the mill.' " (*Juvenile Instructor,* 27:151-2.) That is direct, intimate, and spontaneous.

There were times, though, in sacred circumstances, when the Prophet prayed in a formal way and prayer became a kind of ordinance. One such prayer was delivered at the dedication of the Kirtland Temple. That prayer, recorded in section 109 of the Doctrine and Covenants, has become the model of all subsequent dedicatory prayers. Here was a man who had been given words to say by the Lord—to whom he was to say them. That struck some as circular. But the Prophet here demonstrates that (as President J. Reuben Clark, Jr., puts it) one of the things we should most often pray for is to know what we should most often pray for. (See *Conference Report,* October 1960, p. 90.)

Half, at least, of the prayer process is bringing our souls into receptivity so that we may be powerful listeners and learn the how and when and what of prayer. There is a modern promise that those of us who receive the gospel are "given all things." The Lord's phrase is, "[You are] possessor[s] of all things." "All things" is defined as "the life and the light, the Spirit and the power, sent forth by the will of the Father through Jesus Christ, his Son." And then: "Ye shall ask whatsoever you will in the name of Jesus and it shall be done. But know this, *it shall be given you what you shall ask.*" (See D&C 50:27-30. Italics added.)

But did the Prophet sometimes pray for things never given or for guidance denied him? He did. Like us, he sometimes struggled in vain. For example, the Prophet yearned to know the time of the second coming of Christ. He says he prayed "very earnestly." And the Lord's answer wasn't really an answer, except, "I won't tell you." It was, "Joseph, my son, if thou livest until thou art eighty-five years old, thou shalt see the face of the Son of Man; therefore let this suffice, and trouble me no more on this matter." (D&C 130:15.) So he recorded the only conclusion he could come to: "I believe the coming of the Son of Man will not be any sooner than that time." (D&C 130:17.)

The Lord apparently did not want him—or us—to know the exact time. He wants us to go on living as if his glorious return were tomorrow. Spiritually speaking, that is how prepared we should be. Hence he says over and over, "I come quickly." (See, for example, Revelation 22:20.) But he also wants us, as Wilford Woodruff put it, to "plant cherry trees"—to live our lives in a long-range inspired vision and not in the unauthentic way of some alarmists. They say, "Well, it's all going to blow up in our faces in five years, so why should I plan to go to school?" That is both superficial and escapist.

The Prophet was praying on another occasion to know why his people had to suffer so in Missouri. There is a poignant letter in which he laments: "He will not answer me. He will not answer me." And there were earlier times when he begged the Lord for what the Lord had told him he would not give him.

You remember the instance of Martin Harris. Three times the Prophet prayed for permission to surrender the manuscript. Three times the answer was no. The Prophet, in effect, remonstrated: "But Lord, don't you understand? He mortgaged his farm. His wife is pushing him, Lord. What harm can it do?" Finally permission came. Sometime read Mother Smith's account of how Martin later comes to the Smith house and paces up and down, hesitant to enter. The Prophet sees him through the window and, suspecting the worst, rushes out, "Martin, you haven't lost . . ." Martin nods. For two weeks the Prophet could not be comforted; no one in the family could salve his grief because he felt utterly condemned. The joy of relief that entered his heart when the revelation came, "Repent . . . and thou art . . . again called to the work" (D&C 3:10), was unspeakable! He says in a revelatory account of that day, "those commandments inspired me." Thereafter he wrote, and I think this was a summation of his experience, "I made this my rule, when the Lord commands, do it." (*HC*, Vol. 2, p. 270.) Well, he learned that, but he learned it as we often do—the hard way.

Did the Prophet practice family prayer? On record is an account of a visit of a brother who had never met the Prophet or his family. He was about to knock at the door but hesitated because he heard them singing. Sister Emma was leading the family and guests in a kind of family worship service. Then the Prophet prayed, and the visitor listened breathlessly to what he called "a foretaste of celestial happiness."

The records say Joseph prayed three times a day with his family—morning, noon, and night. (See Alma 34:21.) Beautiful! He once said, citing the book of Daniel, that we should make ourselves "acquainted with those men who . . . pray three times a day toward the House of the Lord." (*HC*, Vol. 3, p. 391.) Daniel did that.

What is the significance of facing the temple? Apparently it is a sacred way of recalling both the promises the Lord has made to us and our promises to him. Thus, when President Wilford Woodruff dedicated the Salt Lake Temple, he offered a specific prayer that when people were assailed with temptation or trouble they might remember the promises of the temple, that they might face the temple, and that the Lord would honor their prayers.

Joseph prayed in his suffering and persecution, but he also prayed in great gratitude. And here is a moving insight. He taught the Saints that they should practice virtue and holiness and "give thanks unto God in the Spirit for whatsoever blessing [they were] blessed with." (D&C 46:32.) How often do we devote an entire prayer simply to thanksgiving and praise? He taught the Saints that if they would learn to be thankful in all things, they would be "made glorious." (D&C 78:19.) Joseph demonstrates an innate and striking capacity for gratitude for even the slightest favor from the Lord or from his fellowmen. I have wept while reading in his journal prayers for his brethren: "Bless Brother So and So, Father, whose hands are blistered from rowing me across the river." Even the smallest favor called out stirring warmth and gratitude.

There are eight different places in the Doctrine and Covenants where the Lord, through the Prophet, uses the expression "pray always." How can we? If "pray always" means vocally, none of us can. But if "pray always" includes the kind of prayer that is wordless and from the heart, we are getting closer. And if it means even more that we are to be in the spirit of prayer regardless of what we may be doing—living prayerfully—then all of us can. In that spirit, the diary of Joseph Smith while on a missionary journey is a continual prayer. "O Lord, seal our testimony to their hearts." "O Lord, comfort my family." The last sentence of his life was a prayer—and the culmination of all others—"O Lord, My God."

But how much do the words matter? Commenting on a New

Testament verse, the Prophet changed a crucial statement on this. It is in Romans. Paul, speaking of how the Spirit can assist us in prayer, says, "The Spirit itself maketh intercession for us with groanings which cannot be uttered." (Romans 8:26.) The Prophet's version is, "The Spirit maketh intercession for us with *striving* which cannot be *expressed*." (*TPJS*, p. 278. Italics added.) When we have enough confidence in the discerning power of the Spirit, we stop worrying so much about forms and are concerned more to open up what is really deep within us, things that we cannot even find words or sounds for. Then the Spirit translates and transmits our strivings. Strivings are different from groanings. We can groan in discouragement and despondency and it will tend to deepen our depression. But strivings are upreaching. We can take our strivings, even those we cannot express, and know that as we silently, prayerfully direct them toward the Father and the Son, the Spirit will translate them perfectly.

In turn, the Spirit can communicate the Lord's response as can no other power. A great confidence and a great freedom can come when we trust the Spirit for that.

Vocal prayer helps our minds stay on the verbal track. But there are advantages also at times to silent prayer and even to a kind of deliberate mind wandering. Let your mind and heart go in the directions they seem impressed to go.

How do we learn to concentrate in the spiritual sense? A remarkable pattern emerges on this and other elements of mighty prayer in the Prophet's instructions to priesthood quorums. Here are his exact words: "I labored with each of these quorums [high priests, seventies, elders, bishops, the Twelve] for some time to bring them to the order which God had shown to me, which is as follows." (*HC*, Vol. 2, p. 391.) This was a special kind of quorum effort in the Kirtland Temple. "The first part to be spent in solemn prayer before God, without any talking or confusion." Apparently, that meant solemn, silent—perhaps whispering—prayer; but no one speaking aloud and no predominant voice.

"And the conclusion with a sealing prayer by President Rigdon." In other words, one man would then pray vocally with and for the entire group. Then "all the quorums were to shout with one accord a solemn hosanna to God and the Lamb with an Amen, Amen and Amen." The "Hosanna Shout" most frequently associated with temple dedications thus had this other sacred personal function. Three times they were to say "Hosanna!" and three times to say "Amen." "Then all take seats and lift up their hearts in silent prayer to God, and if any obtain a prophecy or vision, to rise and speak that all may be edified and rejoice together."

That is a revelatory set of instructions. Even in our own private or secret prayers the spirit of it seems to apply. Note that there is first a concentration—not confusion, but silence. Then a vocal sealing and summarizing prayer. Then a soul-searching outcry of gratitude and need, a manifestation of reverence. And finally a waiting upon the Lord with our hearts open and sensitive and expressing or, in private life, knowing what comes by the Spirit.

What happened when this counsel was enacted? Here is one example. The Prophet says in his journal: "The Quorum of the Seventy enjoyed a great flow of the Holy Spirit. Many arose and spoke, testifying that they were filled with the Holy Ghost, which was like fire in their bones, so that they could not hold their peace, but were constrained to cry hosanna to God." (*HC*, Vol. 2, p. 392.)

And of himself he said: "After these quorums were dismissed, I returned to my home, filled with the Spirit, and my soul cried hosanna to God and the Lamb, through the silent watches of the night; and while my eyes were closed in sleep, the visions of the Lord were sweet unto me and His glory was round about me." (*HC*, Vol. 2, p. 387.)

Much can be learned from that.

But what about those times when we feel unworthy? The

Prophet himself wrote in a letter to Emma: "I call to mind all the past moments of my life and am left to mourn and shed tears of sorrow for my folly." All the prophets, if you study them closely, have known these dark nights, this same struggle, as have other great men and women of our tradition. Nephi, just to name one, writes with such clarity of faith in his first books that you wonder if he ever feared or foundered. But in his psalm he cries out, in effect: "I am led to mourn. When I would rejoice, my soul is bowed down because of my sins." (See 2 Nephi 4:17-19.) And then he prays with great power, "O Lord, encircle me; help me." (See 2 Nephi 4:33.) None of us escape such highs and lows. But would any work be done in the Church if we waited until all of us were perfect?

You remember that the Prophet saw in panoramic vision at least nine of the Twelve in a foreign land. (He doesn't say England, but that is where they eventually went.) He saw them gathered in a circle, without shoes, beaten, tattered, discouraged. Standing above them in the air was the Lord Jesus Christ. And it was made known to the Prophet that Christ yearned to show himself to them, to reach down and lift them. But they did not see him. The Savior looked upon them and wept. We are told by two of the brethren who heard Joseph rehearse that vision that he could never speak of it without weeping himself. Why? Why should he be so touched? Because Christ willingly came to the earth so that all of the Father's family could come to him boldly, knowing that he knows what is taking place in us when we sin, that he knows all our feelings and cares. The greatest tragedy of life is that, having paid that awful price of suffering "according to the flesh that his bowels might be filled with compassion," and being now prepared to reach down and help us, he is forbidden because we won't let him. We look down instead of up.

There may be things in our lives that make us more or less unworthy of certain privileges. But of one thing we are never unworthy: prayer. I add testimony about this. The Prophet

Joseph Smith not only taught it but exemplified it. Regardless of the condition of our soul, we can, we must, go to the Lord. He never closes the door against us; he pleads with us to call upon him when we need him the most. And often that is when we feel least worthy.

I close by bearing witness that we have in the modern Prophet Joseph Smith an example of living, breathing prayer—the intimate touch of prayer, the kind that changes lives. But beyond that the Prophet illustrates for all time that prayer is more than subjective. It isn't just self-hypnosis. It is a plan and pattern whereby we do, in fact, break through the veil and receive the living hand of the living God through Christ. I bear that witness in the name of Jesus Christ. Amen.

Each time after this "Know Your Religion" presentation, questions were submitted in writing. Here are some frequently asked questions and a brief response to each.

1. *How can God the Father hear and answer millions of prayers simultaneously?*

President Hugh B. Brown once began a prayer, "Father, how grateful we are that coming to thee we do not have to make an appointment, work through aides and secretaries, wait our turn, or shorten our visit." He added, "This is incomprehensible to us, O Lord, but we know it is true."

Incomprehensible, yes. But not *totally* incomprehensible. Three glimpses help me. One is that under the glory of the Father, Adam, a mortal man, saw down the stream of time and prophesied what should befall his posterity "unto the last generation." Imagine the inspired inclusiveness of that! Then there are the visions of Enoch and Moses—seeing, discerning, somehow knowing vast world systems and every particle of this earth simultaneously! And then there is the promise that someday we shall "comprehend even God, being quickened in him and by him." (D&C 88:49.) Such quickening, such power will fill our whole bodies with light and turn us into living Urim and Thummim, "where all things for their glory are manifest, past, present, and future." (D&C 130:7.) What is possible for us is actual for him. It is true: not even a sparrow falls to the ground unnoticed.

Further, we must not forget that in the execution of his will through the immensities of space, the Lord is not only aided by the Holy Ghost, which emanates through all space, but by a holy host—a great congregation of the mighty who have come into his likeness and therefore his presence. They help care for the Father's children with living and familial and exquisite care. How many of our prayers are approved by the Father and then executed by those called and ordained of him to carry them out? Someday we will know.

2. *Isn't it possible to fall into autosuggestion in prayer, to convince ourselves that we are talking to someone when we are not, and to claim an "answer" when we are only imposing our own wishes? How do we distinguish?*

Because each of us is somewhat unique in temperament, experience, and approach, each of us has a different "apperceptive mass." Not everyone, for example, as I know from considerable counseling, experiences the influence of the Spirit of the Lord as a "burning in the bosom." For many, the predominant sensation is more generalized "all over"—a kind of lifting elation, or a special illumination of mind that comes with authority and conviction, or a tingling sensation. Thus, the manifestations of the Spirit have many variations. Although we learn and benefit from each other, we need to seek for the kind of experience that is most convincing and trustworthy to us. "If He comes to a little child," the Prophet said, to our comfort, "he will adapt himself to the language and capacity of a little child." (*TPJS*, p. 162.)

In time, our experience has a way of weeding out the more

whimsical prayers, our self-induced and headstrong convictions, and our tendency at times to be "blind guides" of ourselves. In the final analysis the answer here is the same as the answer to any question of how you know one thing from another: only by experience, comparison, and contrast.

3. *Since one cannot always tell the origin of an answer to prayer, how does one avoid tragic mistakes?*

The Prophet had to grow up to ever deeper discernment, and so must we. Three "independent" principles, he said, work upon us: God, ourselves, and the adversary. It is not always easy to know which is which. But of the things of God, the Prophet wrote, "Time, and experience, and careful and ponderous and solemn thoughts can only find them out." (*TPJS*, p. 137.) He left us some helpful revelations on discernment. (See D&C 46 and 50.)

My own experience, inspired by his example, is that a little more silence ("Be still and know that I am God" [D&C 101:16]), a little more listening ("Study it out in your mind; then you must ask me if it be right" [D&C 9:8]), and a little more surrendering (Ye ask amiss that ye may consume it upon your lusts [see D&C 46:9]) will help us find that discernment.

When our impressions are of the mind alone without the heart, or of the heart alone without the mind, they should be carefully reexamined. When both enlightenment of mind— beyond our own deliberation—and burning of heart or feeling occur, we can trust the answer to be of the Lord, and time will vindicate it.

4. *What of the warnings of the Lord to avoid "light-mindedness" (see D&C 88:121) and "loud laughter"? Your stress on "intimacy" suggests we can even come to the Lord with smiles.*

Thankfully, the scriptures make a clear distinction between light-mindedness and lightheartedness. Light-mindedness is not synonymous with all attempts at humor. Light-mindedness is the abuse or ridicule or mocking of sacred things—"making light of" or mocking that which is divine—and there is not much light in the mind that does it.

In the Prophet Joseph's life one can find other kinds of lightness: the deep-breathing laughter of joy and kinship; the quiet laughter of delight at a surprise or privilege; laughing with tears in his eyes at the beautiful antics of a child; and even the wit and wisdom of laughing at himself in the midst of his trials. We do not progress beyond the capacity for joy and refreshment. In fact, the more spiritual-minded we are, the more we grow beyond a static solemnity.

Surely the Father and his Beloved Son are moved in their own perfected character to such manifestations of love. They are not a betrayal of the sacred but one expression of it; not a withdrawal of the Spirit but evidence that the Spirit is there.

We *should* laugh at ourselves and laugh with others. What we are counseled against is laughing at the Lord, his gospel, his sacred things. Such empty laughter will only echo to our sorrow. But the other kind may bring smiles to the eyes of the heavens and bring us back to new energy and sanity.

5. *Can't we be intimate enough to say "you" and "your" in prayer?*

In public prayer with the Saints in meetings and gatherings, we are counseled to maintain the "language of prayer." It helps avoid either the too frequent use of sacred names or a tone that may sound like contemptuous familiarity.

In private prayer, it seems to me, the language to be used is the one that best expresses our depths. And I believe the only irreverence, the only approach that causes the Lord to weep, occurs when we use words to conceal rather than to reveal our most intense feelings and needs. In the end, each of us must pray in the words and style and attitude that seem most authentic to us. At such time there is no such thing as being "too familiar" but only the blasphemy of being too distant, of pretending that aches and confusions and doubts and strivings are not really there. The Lord cannot help us where we most need help until we spill it all out, however starkly. I know from experience that the Father does not make us offenders for our words. Was Christ hiding or measuring his words in the Garden?

6. *If the Lord knows "what things [we] have need of, before [we] ask"* *(Matthew 6:8), and if we are to end our prayers, "Thy will be done" (See* *Luke 22:42), why pray? Either we are asking him to do otherwise than he* *foreknew or intended to do, or we are simply saying, "Do what you would* *have done anyway," which is pointless.*

Both of the assumptions in this question are misapprehensions. First, the Lord's knowledge of our needs includes the knowledge of our need to express them. There are many sound and inspiring reasons for praying that are independent of the response from on high. Moroni counseled the Prophet, "Forget not to pray that thy mind may become strong." (*Improvement Era*, 2:801.) Prayer is mind-strengthening as well as soul-strengthening. It helps us reorder our priorities and bring out into the open what otherwise only stirs and stagnates within. If it were merely a conversation with ourselves, we should have such conversations more often.

But faithful prayer is never just a conversation with oneself. It is one of the co-causes of change in us, in others, and even in the cosmos. We are in a universe of law over which glorious personalities preside. More than fifty times in modern revelation the Lord says, "Seek and ye shall find." Our constant upreach enables him, literally, to bless us. And his intervention and blessing come in perfect justice and mercy as we probe ourselves and prove ourselves in prayer.

As for "thy will be done," this, in the life of Joseph Smith as in the life of Christ, was not a turning *over* of all tasks to the Father but a pulling of the Father's power into life. Prayer was a leaf-by-leaf unfolding of potential, a recovery of their foreappointed mission. Likewise, the greatest prayer for us is a quest for the voluntary agreement, and in some ways an irreversible one, we made before mortality. Thus, "Reveal me to me" should be as constant a prayer as "Reveal thyself to me."

7. *Three questions in one: Is it possible to "weary the Lord"? Are some* *things too trivial to pray about? Are we supposed to be "guided in all* *things"?*

In three instances the Prophet Joseph is told, in effect, "cease to trouble me." But notice in each case he had *already been given the answer.* Even then, I submit, it is impossible to "weary the Lord." He is not that fragile. "Men ought always to pray and not to faint." (D&C 101:81.) To the Nephites the Lord gave instructions to "cease to pray," but he immediately added the command that "they should not cease to pray *in their hearts.*" (3 Nephi 20:1. Italics added.) And the command to pray always (see D&C 10:5) may be combined with "look unto me in every thought" (D&C 6:36).

As for questions of "triviality," how do we know what is trivial and what is not? We may smile patronizingly at a child's prayer about a dog or cat, assuming it is beneath the Lord's notice, and even ours. But are we sure? It matters to the Lord that things matter to us—as it would to any genuine father. And it takes some counsel with him—and some listening as well as asking—to have our sights lifted and to have a deeper sense of what ought to matter. Without communication, without talking with him as well as to him, we are left to guesswork.

That leads to the question of being "guided in all things." The diminution or withdrawal of the Spirit—the dry spells and spiritual deserts we face—are not always due to our unworthiness or to our failure. I am convinced they are part of our mortal trial and the will of the Lord. The Prophet Joseph had to cry out, "O God, where art thou?" (D&C 121:1.) And the Master cried, "Why hast thou forsaken me?" (Matthew 27:46.) To that, one answer may be: "Prove yourself devoted, even when I leave you in the realms of solitude." This insight should not be distorted into the view, "If the Lord has anything to say to me, I suppose he will." If one goes along in indifference, neither seeking nor seeking to live worthy of seeking, he will not find.

House of Glory

We have a temple in Provo now. Many of you have been swept, at least slightly, by the wind that came with the dedication. We have consecrated the oil, so to speak. It's time for us now to administer. And I would like to talk in the spirit of testimony about some of the glorious promises that have been made and some of the essential needs which those promises are designed to answer in our souls.

Let me begin with a story familiar to some of you. It goes back to the dedication of another temple, the Salt Lake Temple, which you will recall took forty years to build. President McKay tells of a man who didn't have money enough even to buy shoes to attend a conference in the Tabernacle. During the conference Brigham Young arose and pled with the brethren that there needed to be more granite brought from the quarry about fifteen miles south. They hauled it mostly by ox team. A man came out from this conference, saw the other brother on the street with a team of

Address given at a ten-stake fireside at BYU, March 5, 1972.

oxen. "Why weren't you there, Brother?" "Uh, my feet. I didn't feel right about going in." "Well, Brother Brigham pled for more people to get granite." "All right," said the brother, "I'll go. Whoa, hah, Buck!" And he started.

President McKay's eyes filled with tears at that simple incident. The reason his name and his image come to mind whenever I think of temples is that it was President McKay who performed the wedding ceremony for my wife, Ann, and myself, and that high privilege was possible for us in part because he had done the same for Ann's parents. He came in his white suit that morning very early on a June day, a white tie, and white hair—you know the majesty of his personality. Somehow we knew then, had we ever doubted it, that no one could speak properly if he spoke evil of the temple, for there before us stood its product.

John the Revelator, who, I believe, was also John the Beloved, visioning the city Jerusalem in glorified state, says, "And there was no temple in it, for the Lamb was the temple of it." And then he adds that not only would the Lamb reign forever, as we sing, but we, having by then been glorified like unto him, would likewise reign forever and ever.

The Salt Lake Temple was dedicated with a sense of sacrifice and gratitude that maybe we have not reached. Forty years! Twenty thousand people gathered just to see the laying of the capstone. And Lorenzo Snow, then one of the Twelve, led them in the hosanna shout that is now familiar to you. And then Wilford Woodruff, who had had a dream years before that he would somehow be involved in the dedication of that temple (and he was, he was the President of the Church) promised that a strict reading of the requirements of worthiness would not be imposed provided the people come feasting and repenting. (That was not a slip of the lip, because the Lord defines fasting and prayer in modern revelation—granting it has its negative side of mourning in some places—as rejoicing and prayer. Fasting is feasting on the Spirit; and somehow not partaking of physical food isn't quite enough. Fasting is a kind of concentration, a kind of pulling ourselves together.)

Well, some eighty thousand people during a twenty-three day period of dedicatory services averaging two thousand each session, were regenerated. President Woodruff's entry in his journal at the end of that year 1893 is: "The greatest event of 1893 was the dedication of the great Salt Lake Temple. Great power was manifest on that occasion." (Mathias Cowley, *Wilford Woodruff* [Salt Lake City: Deseret News Press, 1909], p. 584.)

The scriptural phrase that brings all that into a theme is that we are to receive in temples, through temples, from temples, "power from on high." (See D&C 95:8.) Christ is the source of that power. The temple is his; and every symbol in and out of that sacred structure points toward him and, as a cup carries water, transmits the Spirit of Jesus Christ.

Now to be specific in terms of needs that all of us feel strongly about in our time. It is a characteristic fact that the Lord has commanded the sacrifice of temple-building at the times when apparently our people were least able to build them; and the sacrifice has been immense. But sacrifice "brings forth blessings."

(You may recall that in the 1830s the Brethren kept inquiring. They didn't have our heritage, and they didn't understand even what the word *temple* meant. They kept asking, What is it we are doing? Well, we build a temple. What for? And Joseph Smith told them on one occasion, ". . . nor could Gabriel explain it to your understanding now." But prepare, he told them, for great blessings will come. (See *TPJS*, p. 91.)

Yet in a preparatory revelation (D&C 88) the purposes of the temple are outlined. It's called a house of prayer, it's called a house of fasting, a house of study, a house of learning, a house of glory, and a house of God. Prepare yourselves, it says, "sanctify yourselves . . . and God . . . will unveil his face unto you." (D&C 88:68.)

Let's talk about each of those purposes for a moment.

A house of prayer. "Make yourselves acquainted," said the Prophet once, "with those men who like Daniel pray three times a day toward the House of the Lord." (*HC*, Vol. 3, p. 391.) There is a true principle involved in literally facing the house of God as one prays and as one praises the Lord. The Prophet, as he led a group of faithful Saints through the Nauvoo Temple not yet finished (he did not live to see that day), said to them, "You do not know how to pray, to have your prayers answered." But, as the sister who recorded that brief statement testifies, her husband and she received their temple blessings, and then came to understand what he meant.

A modern leader in our midst, Melvin J. Ballard, said once to a group of young people about solving their problems: "Study it out in your own minds, reach a conclusion, and then go to the Lord with it and he will give you an answer by that inward burning, and if you don't get your answer I will tell you where to go; go to the House of the Lord. Go with your hearts full of desire to do your duty. When in the sacred walls of these buildings, where you are entitled to the Spirit of the Lord, and in the silent moments, the answer will come." (*Utah Genealogical & Historical Magazine*, October 1932, Vol. 23, p. 147.)

For clues to personal experiences behind that statement, you will find that in Elder Ballard's boyhood he often looked up at the Logan Temple and its spires, and was inspired by the spires, and wanted to enter worthily regardless of the costs. That meant for one thing that he never was even tempted to break the Word of Wisdom because he knew that might prevent him from entering that building. I know that his later experiences, many having to do with his ministry, were a derivative often of what he felt, experienced, tasted within the walls of the sanctuary.

If I may be personal, I myself in a critical year away from home and at school drove at times (this was in Los Angeles) to the place they told us there would one day be a temple (it wasn't yet built) just in the feeling that the place might be an added strength to me in prayer. And it proved to be so.

"A house of prayer, a house of fasting, a house of study, a house of learning." One of the men who touched my life was the late Elder John A. Widtsoe, a man who graduated summa cum laude from Harvard after three instead of four years, who was given that last year an award for the greatest depth specializing in his field (which was chemistry); but they also gave an award that year for the student who had shown the greatest breadth of interests, which he also received. Brother Widtsoe has written perceptively about the temple and temple worship. I heard him say in sacred circumstances that the promise was given him by a patriarch when he was a mere boy in Norway: "Thou shalt have great faith, in the ordinances of the Lord's House." And so he did. I've heard him say that the temple is so freighted with depth understanding, so loaded with symbolic grasp of life and its eternal significance, that only a fool would attempt in mere prosaic restatement to give it in a comprehensive way. I've heard him say that the temple is a place of revelation. And he did not divorce that concept from the recognition that the problems you and I have are often very practical, very realistic, down-to-earth problems. He often said, "I would rather take my practical problems to the house of the Lord than anywhere else." And in his book *In a Sunlit Land* he describes a day when, having been frustrated for months, I assume, in trying to pull together a mass of data he had compiled to come up with a formula, he took his companion, his wife, to the Logan Temple to forget his failure. And in one of the rooms of that structure, there came, in light, the very answer he had heretofore failed to find. Two books on agrarian chemistry grew out of that single insight—a revelation in the temple of God.

The temple is not just a union of heaven and earth. It is the key to our mastery of the earth. It is the Lord's graduate course in subduing the earth, which, as only we understand, ultimately will be heaven—this earth glorified.

A house of learning? Yes, and we learn more than about the earth. We learn *ourselves.* We come to comprehend more deeply, in an environment that surrounds one like a cloak, our own identity, something of the roots that we can't quite reach through memory but which nevertheless are built cumulatively into our deepest selves—an infinite memory of conditions that pre-date memory. The temple is the catalyst whereby the self is revealed to the self.

There was a period when I was required as an officer in the Ensign Stake to go every Friday to the temple. It was not a burden as I had thought it would be. It became instead my joy. Slowly, because of that regularity, I was trusted with certain assignments in the temple. This meant that I could walk into the temple annex and they would all say, "Good morning, Brother Madsen"; and I wouldn't even have to show my recommend. Not only that, but I had the privilege to sit for hours in the chapel of the annex or elsewhere, contemplative, reading occasionally, but trying to absorb, trying to breathe the air that is heavier than air in that place. There I would meditate about my critical problems, which had to do with decisions about my life's work, decisions about the girl I should marry, and other struggles in how to cope. There were, I testify, times when I learned something about me; there were times when peace came in a decision, and I knew that that peace was of God.

The temple is a house of learning. And it is intended that therein we not simply learn *of* or *about* Christ, but that we come to *know* him. It has always impressed me that in the Inspired Version the classic passage about the hereafter and how many will say, "Lord, Lord, did we not do this and that?" is rendered more fittingly than in the King James Version. The King James Version says that Christ will respond, "I never knew you." The Inspired Version renders it, "You never knew me."

This is the gospel of Jesus Christ. This is the Restored Church of Jesus Christ. This is the Church that teaches us that we can have a direct and immediate living relationship with the Living Christ. And we inscribe on temples, "Holiness to the Lord," "The House of the Lord." He told us, and it isn't qualified, that as respects our preparation, "all the pure in heart that come into it shall see God." Orson Pratt points out that this promise specifically relates with a temple not yet built, a temple to be erected in the center City, the New Jerusalem, wherein someday Christ actually will dwell; and wherein, therefore, any who enter will meet him. But again, Brother John A. Widtsoe, Brother George F. Richards, President Joseph Fielding Smith, and others have borne witness that the promise is more extensive than that; and that it applies now. It is a promise that we may have a wonderfully rich *communion* with him. *Communion!* That is to say that we are not simply learning propositions *about*, but that we are in a participative awareness *with*.

Occasionally we struggle in amateur research in Church history to understand what kind of a portrait, in terms of sheer physical appearance, one could draw of Christ if we simply utilized what modern witnesses have said about their glimpses of him. It's an impressive portrait. But one thing perhaps we sometimes neglect in that curiosity is an awareness or a seeking for an awareness of his personality, of those subtler realities that we already recognize in other persons in all variations but which have been perfected in him. What would it be like to be in his presence, not simply in terms of what you would see but what you would feel? "Listen," he says, to give us one clue, and these passages were included by our prophet in the recent dedicatory prayer in Provo, "to him . . . who is pleading your cause before [the Father], saying: Father, behold the sufferings and death of him who did no sin [that is to say, committed none, but he knows them, for he experienced temptation to do them all], in whom thou wast well pleased; behold the blood of thy Son which was shed, . . . Wherefore, Father, spare these my brethren." (D&C 45:3, 4.) That's a glimpse of the compassion that one comes to feel in communion—the feeling with, the feeling for, that he has. He is the one Personality, if there are no others (and I dare predict that for many of us the time will come when we will feel there are no others), of whom it cannot truthfully be said: "You don't know me. You don't understand me. You don't care about me." Because of what he went through, all three statements would be eternally false. And he has had us sacrifice to build sacred houses where the linkage of his heart, his "bowels of compassion" can merge with ours.

The temple is a place of learning to know him.

And now the phrase "a house of glory, a house of God." One of the most tender moments of my spiritual life was the day a woman, Rose Wallace Bennett, authoress of the *Gleaner Sheaf*, told me that as a little girl she was present in the dedicatory services of the Salt Lake Temple. She described also the day Wilford Woodruff had a birthday, his ninetieth, when it was a little girl's privilege to take forward to him in the Tabernacle ninety roses in a setting of some eight thousand children between the ages of eight and twelve, all in white. They had gathered to honor him; and then as he had come into the building (under some pretense that there was need of an organ repair), they arose and sang, "We Thank Thee, O God, for a Prophet." She could not talk about what it felt like to see his tears, or again, what it was like to be in the temple, without herself weeping. But what she said to me was: "Young man, my father brought me to the edge of City Creek Canyon where we could look down on the temple. I testify to you that there was a light around the temple, and it was not due to electricity."

There are such phrases in all the authentic literature that has to do with temple dedications: "light," "glory," "power." Even nonmembers of the Church at Kirtland came running, wondering what had happened. They wondered if the building was on fire. It was; but with what the Prophet called "celestial burnings," the downflow of the power of the Living God, like encircling flame as on the day of Pentecost. A prayer for that had been offered by the Prophet and by his father, and it was fulfilled. (D&C 109:36, 37.)

What is glory? Well, it is many things in the scriptures. One strand of meaning is often neglected. If we can trust one Hebrew student, the Hebrew word equivalent to glory, *Kabod*, refers in some of its strands to physical presence. Just as a person says in common parlance today, "he was there in all his glory," so the Old Testament often uses this word for God. In the Psalm that refers to the glory (Psalm 8) there are two changes that are crucial. King James reads, "Thou hast made [man] a little lower than the angels, and hast crowned him with glory and honour." Probably what that verse said originally was, "Thou hast made [man] a little lower than the *Gods*, and hath crowned him with a *physical body* and with honor." This is the truth. The body is a step *up* in the scales of progression, not a step down. God is God because he is gloriously embodied; and were he not so embodied, he would be less than God.

The privilege of the house of God is in effect to have our physical beings brought into harmony with our spirit personalities. And I have read, but cannot quote perfectly, only paraphrase, the testimony of President Lorenzo Snow to the effect that this is the only way—I repeat, the only way—that the knowledge locked in our spirit can become part of this flesh; thus occurs that inseparable union, that blending, which makes possible celestial resurrection. It is as if, if I may mix the figure, we are given in the house of God a patriarchal blessing to every organ and attribute and power of our being, a blessing that is to be fulfilled in this world and the next, keys and insights that can enable us to live a godly life in a very worldly world, protected—yes, even insulated—from the poisons and distortions that are everywhere.

That is the temple. And the glory of God, his ultimate perfection, is in his house duplicated in us, provided we go there in a susceptible attitude.

Let me turn to a few remarks about the how of susceptibility. Listening once in Los Angeles to the plea of President McKay, stake president after stake president pledged contributions to make possible the building of the Los Angeles Temple. They committed. And then he arose and delivered a masterful discourse, maybe the greatest I have ever heard on the subject of temples. In shorthand I jotted down one paragraph which I'm going to quote, but before I do so, let me give this explanation. He told of a girl, a girl, I found later, who was his niece and therefore felt confident in confiding in him. Earlier that year she had been initiated in a sorority, and not long thereafter she had "gone through the temple" (as we say)—I wish that verb could be improved—"going through the temple." I wish we could somehow speak of the temple going through *us*. I wish that my children had not been confused—it's my fault that they were—when my wife and I used to say to them, "We are going to *do* sealings." They thought that we would take a stepladder and a bucket. It's a kind of Mormon activism to talk about "temple work." There is a sense of course, in which it is work; but too rarely do we speak of "temple worship," which can send us back to our work changed.

A man of God in the temple said in my hearing, "I wonder if the dead are blessed as much as the living by the temple." I am impatient with people who are impatient in the temple. I am distressed when someone sits behind me with a stop-watch and keeps saying, "They're five minutes behind. Move! Move! Move!" Isn't there *one* place we can go and leave our watch in the locker and rejoice if there are delays, and embrace what is there for us?

Well, on the occasion in Los Angeles, President McKay stopped everyone by saying: "This young lady came to me. She had had both experiences, but said she had been far more impressed with her sorority." We gasped as you did. President McKay was a master of the pause. He let that wait a minute and then said: "Brothers and sisters, she was disappointed in the temple. Brothers and sisters, I was disappointed in the temple."

But then he finished his sentence. "And so were you." Then no one gasped. He had us. "*Why* were we?" he asked. And then he named some of the things. We were not prepared. How could we be, fully? We had stereotypes in our minds, faulty expectations. We were unable to distinguish the symbol from the symbolized. We were not worthy enough. We were too inclined quickly to respond negatively, critically. And we had not yet seasoned spiritually. Those are my words, but they cover about what he said. I will give you the quotation verbatim.

He said: "Brothers and sisters, I believe there are few"—and I remind you this was a man at that time eighty years of age who had been in the temple every week for some fifty years, which gave him, I thought, some right to speak—"I believe there are few, even temple workers, who comprehend the full meaning and power of the temple endowment. Seen for what it is, it is the step-by-step ascent." (I pause to remind you of both strands of meaning: assent, agreement, consent, covenant; but also ascent, rise.) "It is the step-by-step ascent into the Eternal Presence. If our young people could but glimpse it, it would be the most powerful spiritual motivation of their lives."

When he said that, I felt it. I had myself been a critic; had made up my mind that some things were trivial, offensive. But that day the Lord touched me, and I decided that I would not speak again against the house of the Lord. I would not jest. I would not assume I knew better than the prophets. I would listen. And I would repent. And I would hope that someday I could testify as did that noble man. In time there was far more opened up to me than I had ever dreamed.

But there were three things amiss in me, and I dare to suppose these may apply to some of you. First, I hadn't even read the scriptures carefully about the temple. It had not occurred to me that there are over three hundred verses, by my count, in the Doctrine and Covenants alone that talk about the temple and the "hows," if you will, of preparation. I had not read what the

Brethren had said to help us. I was unaware that there were such materials as *The House of the Lord* by Elder James E. Talmage (a very difficult book, but focus on the parts having to do with today and you, and it can help); that remarkable compilation of Elder Widtsoe, a book called *A Rational Theology*, but with it his excellent essay "Temple Worship," which some stake presidents here at BYU still distribute upon request as preparation; Elder Harold B. Lee's *Youth and the Church*, three chapters dealing with this; Archibald F. Bennett's lucid manual *Saviors on Mount Zion*, rich with nuggets. Well, I hadn't even looked.

Second, I was, I am afraid, afflicted with various kinds of unworthiness and not too anxious to change all that. Oh, we talk of it and we aspire. We want change, but we don't want it enough. We are (and I don't laugh at poor Saint Augustine for saying this) like Saint Augustine who said in a prayer, "Oh God, make me clean, but not yet." We talk of sacrifice. The one the Lord asks of *you now* is the sacrifice of your sins—the hardest thing in the world to give up. There's still a certain bittersweet enjoyment. But his promise is crystal clear. "If you will purify yourselves, sanctify yourselves, I will bless you." And I'm afraid the postscript is: "And if you don't, I can't."

The third point is that I had a built-in hostility to ritual and to symbolism. I was taught, with good intention I have no doubt, by people both in and out of the Church, that we don't believe in pagan ceremony; we don't believe in all these procedures and routines; that's what they did in the ancient apostate church; we've outgrown all that. Well, we're in effect throwing out the baby with the bath. We're not against ordinances. God has revealed them anew. And I suspect they are as eternal as are what we often call eternal laws. There are certain patterns or programs, certain chains if you will, of transmission which are eternal. Ordinances tie in with those, if they are not identical with them. God has so decreed, but that decree is based upon the very ultimate nature of reality. You *cannot* receive the powers of godliness, says the scripture, except through the ordinances. (See D&C 84:20.) Well, that hadn't ever entered my soul. I thought our sacraments were a bit of an embarrassment and that sometime we could do away with them. One day it suddenly became clear to me—this is the Lord's pattern of our nourishment. We need spiritual transformation. We can eat, if you will, receive, drink—and the Lord uses all those images—the Living Fountain through ordinances.

Well, I pray that you will reach out for what is written, reach out for repentance, and reach out in the recognition that the ordinances are channels of living power.

Some of you were quite conscious of the dedicatory prayer, and perhaps you sensed the power that was poured out as it was uttered. Those prayers from the beginning have been given by revelation, and that fact has been puzzling to some. How can the Lord reveal a prayer to offer to him who has revealed it? Well, there's nothing contradictory in that. One cannot know fully what to pray until he receives guidance from the Lord. "He that asketh in the Spirit," says modern revelation, "asketh according to the will of God." (D&C 46:30.) You must listen in order to know what to say. And prayers that are all ask and no listen are not very effective.

The temple is the place where you can come to understand what the Lord would have you ask. And it is the place where you can ask, in silence, in joy, in earnestness.

Years ago, I was involved in the Ensign Stake Genealogical Committee. We held a series of firesides. The climactic of six was given by President Joseph Fielding Smith. (Here is, by the way, an interesting point: six of our Presidents have been temple presidents, he being one.) The last lecture was given on temple marriage. But the week before that I had been asked to speak on vital temple purposes. I struggled with that. I was talking to young people. What was most remarkable came toward the end of what I said. I wanted somehow to let them know that my own assurance about marriage had come within the walls of the temple; that, in effect, my wife and I had had a temple courtship as well as a temple marriage. It was in the temple that I later gave her a ring.

But I didn't want to acknowledge publicly that I was going to marry this girl. That had not yet been said in private, and therefore I didn't think it should be said in public. But there came down on me that night (and I have a tape-recording that tells the story) such a witness that I announced, "The Lord has made known to me that I am to be married, and to whom." She was on the front row, sitting next to my father. It came as a bit of a surprise to him, too. There was much salt water. Have you heard Pasternak's phrase, "Be so close to those you love that when they weep you taste salt"? I did. I gasped, though, at what I had said and wanted somehow to alter, qualify, call back, change. That was shown in several seconds of silence. Then at last all I could do was say, "In the name of the Lord, amen," and sit down.

Now what has that to do with anything? This. I testify that the Lord's Spirit has prompted you individually, most of you here tonight, that that city set on a hill, that temple, is yours; that something about it can change your lives; that you need to reach for it, to honor it, if need be to sacrifice for it, even your sins. And some of you have fought against that, as I fought against it, because it means change, maybe some painful change. But I witness to you, that is the Spirit of God. This valley will never be the same now that that building stands there day and night as witness. And *you* will be changed if you will honor the promptings and let the Lord have you.

I bear testimony that he lives. And I bear testimony that he *is* in his temples, that he ministers personally, manifests himself unto the faithful therein; and that entering the house of God, whatever else may happen, is equivalent to being in the locks of the Panama Canal; and while the ship is stopped from the rush of the earlier voyage, water comes up and surrounds it and then it leaves eastward on a new ocean.

I testify that the power of Christ is in his sanctuary and that it's intended that all of you drink deeply, receive powerfully, and then testify worthily of that glorious truth. In the name of Jesus Christ. Amen.

Index

infinite memory of man unlocked through, 39

man endowed with power to withstand Satan through, 45

metaphors of the universe, 36

no solitude in, 47

not to be altered, 42

ordinary made extraordinary through, 38

power of godliness manifested in, 41

signs of God and Christ, 37-38

signs of reality, 37

two worlds connected through, 41

understanding of, 40

unifying of self through, 39

unifying power of, 46

universal and particular combined through, 41

pattern of nourishment, 104

- P -

Paul, on Abraham, 55

Perfect, command to become, 3

Personality, 35

three kinds of, 29

Planting and harvesting, image in D&C, 25

Plato, 39

on learning as recollection, 19

on preexistence of soul, 19

Polanyi, M., on knowledge, 34

Positivism, 70

Power-ethic, 71

Pratt, Helaman, call to Mexico, 54-55

Pratt, Orson, on future temple in Jerusalem, 99

on every spirit having seen Christ in preexistence, 19

on no man being without a gift, 20

Pratt, Parley, P., on innate feeling to kindred spirits, 18-19

Prayer, addressing the Father in, 79

a kind of ordinance, 79

and guidance in all things, 91

autosuggestion and, 87

avenue to God and Christ, 86

constant, 82

content of, 80-81, 105

discerning the Lord's Spirit and one's own desires, 87-88

expressing of, 82-83

facing temple during, 81-82, 96

family, 81

formality of, 79

frequency of, 81

fruits of honest, 84

God hears every, 86

God's omniscience and, 90

hallmark of, 78

honesty in, 26-27

Joseph Smith and prayer in sacred grove, 77

language of, 89-90

length of, 78-79

man prays not alone, 77

not wearying to the Lord, 91

petitions of, 79

purpose of, 90

quorum, in Kirtland Temple, 83-84

requests of, not always granted, 80

structure of, 84

triviality and, 91

vocal, 83

worthiness and, 84-86

Preexistence, man's choice to come to earth, 19

memory of, to be restored, 20

exquisite condition of man in, 17

personal ties before earth life, 19

purpose of preexistent preparation, 18

Priesthood, duty and burden of, 53

to try men, 53

Principles, three independent, 88

Prophets, purpose of, 5

Psychologism, 70

Pulsipher, John, on duty, 54

- Q -

Quickened, meaning of, 26

- R -

Random Harvest, James Hilton, 15

film version, allegory of our life, 16

film version of book, 15

story of man with a lost memory, 16

Rasmussen, Ellis, comment on Mount Moriah, 50

Rational Theology, A, John A. Widtsoe, 104